Live Your Playlist

How to Get Your S#&! Together

One Song at a Time

Andrea Vecchio

ISBN: 0692289046
ISBN 13: 9780692289044

This book is dedicated to my mom and dad. You bought me my first records, my first tapes, and my first CDs. You exposed me to the music that touched my soul. And you taught me to be my best self through your love, guidance, and the examples that you set every day of my life.

To the musicians, songwriters, and singers who inspired me. Thank you for the gift of your music. It healed my soul.

And to anyone who has lost faith, confidence, and hope. My hope is that these words and stories will help you feel empowered and find a way to heal and shine again!

I have a new love for that glittering instrument, the human soul. It is a lovely and unique thing in the universe. It is always attacked and never destroyed—because "Thou mayest."
John Steinbeck, *East of Eden*

Author's Note

This book is a work of nonfiction combined with advice from the author. The names of some characters have been changed, and some are composites of various people, experiences, and locations. This is a recollection of stories from my life and is written as I remember the events, to the best of my ability. In the end, even the painful stories have an empowering lesson. And that is ultimately the goal of this book: to be empowered through positive and negative experiences. For that I am grateful to all the characters and experiences in this book.

Table of Contents

Foreword

Being a part of "The Magnificent Seven", the first American women's gymnastics team to win an Olympic gold medal, changed my life indefinitely and afforded me the opportunity to meet fascinating people all over the world.

I think back to the first time I met Andrea Vecchio—a keen, slender brunette with hazel eyes. It was 2007, and I appeared on her Cleveland morning show where she interviewed me about a charity I was involved with. Andrea was a seasoned veteran in television, and I was instantly captivated by her humility as she removed herself from her chair to greet me prior to the interview. She was warm, and I felt especially comfy with her from the outset. As we chatted about the upcoming segment, I thought to myself, "I hope we can become friends".

Very quickly, we formed a meaningful relationship. Patchy lunches soon evolved into steady nights of vino and long walks sharing moments of triumph, secret petitions of our hearts, and our self-doubts. It was on one of our dinners where Andrea first mentioned her dream to author a book. Her tone was both genuine and resolute, and she took the leap of faith.

Andrea's story is a journey toward self-empowerment and healing. **Live Your Playlist** is funny, revealing, and poignant. After losing her job in television, and filing for unemployment, Andrea reached a fork in the road moment regarding her life and purpose. She boldly details what she's discovered through a health scare, interviewing A-list celebrities, and turbulent interpersonal relationships. Andrea's candid accounts touch the heart and go beyond everyday storytelling. **Live Your Playlist** uses the emotional triggers of music to evoke heavy-duty feelings to help empower. Her writing style is distinctive, her words are witty, and I believe in her heartfelt message.

Each chapter is inspired by a song that has helped revive Andrea from a dismal, insecure, or uncertain place. From Chapter One, "Chasing a Hollywood Dream" through the emotional roller coaster of Chapter Four, "He Loves Me, He Loves Me Not" to the compelling final chapter of "The Power of Your Army," you'll find yourself laughing out loud all the while having your heart touched by a journey that teaches us to heal from life's deepest scars. Andrea demonstrates how she's chosen to rise above it all. Please enjoy the inspiring, entertaining, and heartwarming voyage of **Live Your Playlist**!

Dominique Moceanu
Olympic Gold Medalist
New York Times Best-Seller, Off Balance
Cleveland, Ohio

Introduction

I never thought I would write a self-help book. During my years as a television talk show host, every time a self-help author was booked on my show, I asked the producers to give the interview to one of the other hosts. Honestly, I just couldn't get into that genre of writing. So I find it ironic that I've now written a self-help book mixed with storytelling. I guess that makes me a literary convert. We all experience events in our lives that change our course, reshape our thoughts, and sometimes force us to take a leap of faith.

When I started sending my book out to literary agents, the responses were similar across the board. In so many words, they all told me that I was a gifted writer with an inspiring voice. But they added that because I was not famous, I would be a tough sell to a big publishing company. I could have given up on my dream of publishing this book. But that didn't seem like a good idea. And so I said, "Fuck it. I'm going to find a way to get my book into the hands of readers who will hopefully connect with my stories."

But that's not where this story begins.

The idea for this book came at a time when I had nothing but time. I learned during this period of life that time can be your friend or your enemy. Time can heal. But it can also make the waiting game of life feel like slow torture, plagued by endless bouts of self-doubt and questions about who you are and where you're going. I was jobless and calculating how many months I could go without working before I was broke. I wasn't sure where my next paycheck would come from or if I would find a job in my line of work. My days of unemployment were filled with wondering what I wanted to be when I grew up.

The problem was that I was already grown up, and I didn't know the answer to my question. Professionally, I was in limbo. Personally, there was no man to love and no children to call my own. I only had the fading dream that I might have both someday. My health was in question for the first time in my life, which caused sleepless nights. My confidence and self-worth were shaken. Worry and panic about my future became all-too-familiar feelings. I used to believe that when everything was falling apart, there was one thing to keep a person moving forward—hope. I was losing hope. When I looked at myself in the mirror, I saw the reflection of a thirtysomething-year-old woman who was jobless, with no relationship, no children, and a health scare that could be life changing. I felt hollow and numb. The girl looking back at me was a girl who failed. But she was also a woman who felt the expectations of others to succeed again. As I was sizing up my wounds, I decided that I had a choice to make. I could continue to feed my self-doubt and ask, "How did this happen to me?" and "What is the purpose of that girl in the mirror?" Or I could reacquaint myself with the confident, intelligent, and motivated woman I knew existed somewhere behind the layers of self-pity and hopelessness.

Have you ever reached a point of despair in your life? A time when you've lost who you are, the direction in which you're going, and the person you thought you were meant to be? You once had a plan. You could see your future. And at times you were living your dream. But then one event, one moment in time, left you feeling as if your dreams and goals had been erased from existence.

Maybe you feel worthless. Maybe you feel lost. Maybe you feel as if the map of your life has suddenly become a blank canvas. And you don't know how to begin to dream in color, let alone black and white. Why? The reason is because you don't know how to define your new beginning. You can't see it clearly. In fact, you can't see it at all. I know that feeling. And I'm writing this book to show you the steps it takes to fill up your blank canvas in a way that gives you purpose and makes you feel whole again. It's a lot easier to give up on yourself. It takes no work to do that. But if you choose to work on *you*, to heal from your pain and to have the courage to face rejection time and time again, you'll realize that putting hard work into yourself is the most rewarding work of all.

When I was at my lowest point in life, I made a conscious choice to work on myself physically and heal my wounds. I started with simple things like going to church again after years of low-record attendance. I ate well and paid attention to the foods that I put into my body, all while believing that everything in moderation applies to all food groups, including Lay's Wavy potato chips and chocolate-covered anything. I found pleasure in cooking new recipes every night and experimented with foods that I didn't know how to pronounce. I made a habit of flossing daily because I was raised by parents who told me that good dental hygiene was key to my overall health.

While I was healing, I decided to stay away from alcohol. Why would I stay away from a delicious liquid that can often numb pains of the heart? Because drinking too much impaired my ability to make good decisions and tempted me to make a phone call that I shouldn't make (we've all been there after a bad breakup). It was a successful decision that lasted for eight months. When I regained my emotional strength, I enjoyed red wine and cocktails again. And I never made that phone call that I knew I would later regret once I had a clear mind. My social hours were only spent with people who cared about me and brought happiness and wisdom into my life. And most importantly, I worked out every day. My workouts allowed me to clear my mind, and ultimately I gained clarity and insight into my personal struggles. Whenever I began to feel insecure, angry, fearful, or despair, I put on my running shoes and pushed "play" on my playlist. I was dedicated to my workouts as though my life depended on them.

At first, my workouts were just walks around the neighborhood in which I grew up. There was something comforting about the smells and sights of my childhood playground, a place of happy times and good memories. My walks turned into easy jogs. And then I added a little bit of running. I never missed an opportunity to carve out this time in the day for myself. Even on days when I didn't want to get out of bed. And believe me, those days happened. But I forced myself to peel off my bedcovers and lace up my running shoes every day. My workouts were a daily ritual. But I could only do this ritual with the help of my playlist. Every song on my playlist was chosen with a purpose. Every lyric on the playlist had a meaning. Music is a universal language that helps us express our emotions. Whether it's the song you chose on your wedding day to express your love for your partner or a sappy love song that you play over and over again after a breakup. And sometimes there's that one song that you and your friends play when you're going out on the town. It's your anthem for the night! Music helps us express what we are feeling in our souls.

When I put on my earphones and pressed "play" on my playlist, my emotional journey began. Sometimes I would cry on my walks. And sometimes I would get angry on a run. But during this time, a time that was just for me, I talked myself through my pain. The artists I chose ranged from Eminem and Madonna to Christina Aguilera and Miranda Lambert. My healing was happening through the music. I was living my playlist. Searching for answers. Reflecting on my past. Figuring out what I didn't like about myself. Coming to terms with some painful experiences in my life. And sorting through poor choices. But I was also reconnecting with the things that truly made me happy. And I became reacquainted with my strengths. I was on a journey. I want to share that journey with you because while the details of our stories may be different, I believe the emotions and pains we've experienced will be our connection. My hope is that these stories and lessons will empower you. It's time for you to live your playlist. It's not all pretty. But let's be honest, it isn't for any of us if we truly *live*.

one

Chasing a Hollywood Dream

Playlist Song & Artist: "Born This Way" Lady Gaga

Has there even been that moment in your life when everything seemed perfect? I mean, maybe you weren't a Rolling Stone, but you felt like a rock star. That moment happened for me. I was hosting a television talk show in my hometown of Cleveland, flying all over the world interviewing the biggest stars on the planet, going to award shows in Los Angeles and sitting a few tables away from Brad Pitt, Angelina Jolie, Matt Damon, and Steven Spielberg. I was eating at the finest restaurants in the city and had all of the popular chefs' cell phone numbers on speed dial. During a typical work weekend, I would sit down and conduct one-on-one interviews with A-list celebrities like George Clooney, Julia Roberts, Robert De Niro, and Denzel Washington. After many failed relationships, I met a man who, in many ways, seemed too good to be true. We started making plans to get married and start a family of our own. I would drive into work every morning with a smile on my face. And looking up to the sky I would say, "Thank you so much for my life." I felt unbelievably happy and lucky.

And then, just like that, it ended. I lost my job. The man in my life left me. I was thirty-six years old, unmarried, and childless. I had a huge lump on my back next to my spine that I ignored for over a year. And I had no idea what the mound was below the surface of my skin. I only knew it wasn't supposed to be there. The lump was getting bigger and required surgery. But no job meant no health insurance. I couldn't get anyone in television to hire me. And I wondered if I would ever have a job that I was proud of again.

I had to move home with my parents because it was the only living space that was rent free. Meanwhile I lied to everyone about where I was living because I was so embarrassed about my failures. Many people knew I lost my job, but I didn't want them to think I lost my independence too. As the months passed and the money from my checking account was about to run out, I had to do something I never thought I would do in my life. I filed for unemployment. I was a college graduate. I paid my dues in my profession for years. I worked my way to the top. I even owned really nice purses. And then overnight, I seemed to lose everything. Except for the nice purses.

It truly seemed to be one stroke of bad luck after another. But it took me on a journey. A journey with a lot of pain. You've heard the phrase "What doesn't kill you makes you stronger." Well, when you're going through hard times, those words just feel like bullshit. And the shit was pouring all over me. While I felt like I had nothing, the one thing that I did have was a lot of time. Free time to do whatever I wanted. I couldn't afford to drink my time away with Caymus and Silver Oak. I was lactose intolerant, so the proverbial pint of Ben & Jerry's ice cream was out of the question. And so, without my wine and Cherry Garcia, I started walking every day. I went far. Not like Tom Hanks in *Forrest Gump* far. But I traveled until my legs were numb. My workouts became my job. And my playlists were chosen to reflect my struggles. I became enlightened on this journey. But before I share all of it, including the parts I'm hesitant to write about, let's start at the beginning...

As I was wrapping up my junior year of college at The Ohio State University, I had no idea what I wanted to do after I graduated and earned my degree. My Grandma Mary told me, "You should be a news lady like Wilma Smith."

Wilma Smith was the grand dame of Cleveland news. She was a legendary anchorwoman off the shores of Lake Erie. Wilma was tall, beautiful, blond, and classy. Everyone in town knew her name. And even if you didn't watch her every day, if you were from Cleveland, you knew Wilma Smith. She was a fixture in a town that likes familiarity. Wilma was a local celebrity, and I guess my grandma Mary thought I could end up like her. My loving grandmother was blind to the fact that I had no hairstyle, owned only one suit from Ann Taylor, and needed to lose some of the pizza pounds I gained at Ohio State because I heard that the camera adds ten pounds. I needed TV news hair and a better wardrobe! But first I needed a television connection.

My television contact came soon after my grandmother's epiphany about my future career. My mom was attending a luncheon one afternoon at a country club in town. The guest speaker was a female news anchor at one of the local television stations. My mom approached the speaker after the event and inquired about what her daughter needed to do to get into television. The anchor's suggestion was to start with an internship. After my mom collected contact phone numbers at the luncheon, I made some calls to a television producer and human resources manager at one of the local stations. After a few persistent phone calls, I landed a summer internship on a local talk show.

The show covered everything from entertainment and big news stories to fitness and cooking demonstrations. My internship was very hands on and taught me a tremendous amount about the production of a live television show. At nineteen years old I could confidently say I was having the best summer of my life! I met soap stars and musicians, went to lunch with the show's producers, and got to be on TV for a fashion show. I was responsible for finding topic ideas, preparing guests for the live show, and making sure that the hosts and producers had everything they needed for the broadcast. I felt so cool being a part of this team! But more importantly, I knew I had found my calling. I was going to be in television! And when some of the producers of the show encouraged me to pursue a reporting career, my dream of being in front of the camera began.

As with most careers, you start by paying your dues and doing entry-level work. After my internship and graduation, I was hired to be an associate producer on the same talk show. This meant that I booked guests for the show, wrote interviews for the hosts, and yes, I also made the occasional coffee run. I was paid six dollars an hour for this job. But the money didn't matter to me. I was thrilled to be working in my chosen field and willing to work hard to reach a point of professional and financial success. I worked long hours. And I was committed to delivering my best work, no matter how long it took me to complete the job.

My new position allowed me to have a key to the television station. I would go into the station on my days off and work on my demo reel. A demo reel is an edited video that showcases a variety of a journalist's best work on camera. If I wanted to be hired for an on-air job, I needed to have a demo reel. As an associate producer, I was working behind the camera. So I had to "fake" my on-air work for my demo reel. I tagged along with reporters and photographers when they covered stories for the broadcast. And during this time the photographers would record tape of me pretending to be a reporter. I did this process more often than I can count. Every time, I got better in front of the camera. And then it happened, the opportunity of a lifetime for a young, aspiring reporter.

The entertainment reporter on our show was scheduled to fly to Los Angeles to interview some actors for a new film. When this reporter was told that there were no A-list celebrities to interview, the reporter wasn't happy. The interview list didn't include any actors who were considered "promotable names." Meaning if they weren't the lead story on *Entertainment Tonight*, on the cover of *Us Weekly*, *TMZ*'s hottest story of the day, or an Oscar winner, they weren't relevant. That's not my theory. That's the business. That's the entertainment world. And our entertainment reporter was questioning whether or not this work trip was a waste of time. I recall the reporter asking me if I knew the name Russell Crowe. I replied that I did not. Russell Crowe was listed as the lead actor of this new film and was at the top of the interview list. And at this point in time, he was not a household name.

After meeting with the show's executive producer, our entertainment reporter decided that this work trip to Los Angeles would not be worthwhile. It was a predicament for our executive producer. Our show had made a commitment to the movie studio to send a reporter. And now that reporter refused to do the job. What were we supposed to do now? The solution definitely worked in my favor! The phone on my rickety work desk rang. It was my boss.

I recall the quiet tone of his voice saying, "Can you come to my office for a minute?" I made the ten-step walk to his office. Shut the door behind me. And I took a seat across from his desk. My life was about to change. The executive producer of our show was sending me to Los Angeles to interview a few Hollywood actors, including the unknown Russell Crowe.

For some reason my boss had confidence in me, a young, twenty-two-year-old rookie. My boss knew I had bigger dreams than my six-dollar-an-hour job. When the executive producer sat me down in his office to give me my first travel assignment,

I remember that he told me this would be a huge opportunity to practice my interview skills and use the interviews on my demo tape. He told me that he was confident I would represent our station well and conduct a smart interview. My boss's confidence in me gave me confidence in myself. This man gave me my first big shot in television, for which I will always be grateful. The next day I was on a plane to Los Angeles to interview the cast of the upcoming movie *The Insider*.

Russell Crowe was the lead actor in the film, but he was not known as "The Gladiator" yet. It didn't matter to me that he wasn't a famous star. This was my big chance to prove that I could be a good interviewer. To prepare for my interview, I researched everything that I could find on the Internet about Russell Crowe. The more I read, the more nervous I became. It appeared there was a common theme in Russell Crowe's interviews. I noticed that if a reporter asked Russell Crowe a stupid question, in so many words he told the reporter that it was a stupid question. Uneasiness set into my psyche, and a voice in my head told me that I was a twenty-two-year-old kid who would probably ask a stupid question! But I fought the voice in my head and reminded myself that this was an amazing opportunity and I had to meet the challenge.

The assignment that took me from Cleveland to Los Angeles is called a movie junket. It's a time when regional and foreign press gather to screen a film, interview the cast and director of the movie, and then take those interviews back to their home markets to play on the air. In *The Insider*, Russell Crowe plays a middle-aged man named Jeffrey Wigand. Wigand was a whistleblower on the big tobacco industry. The movie is based on a true story. And even though I wasn't a film critic at the time, I thought Russell Crowe was outstanding in the role. My interviews were held the day after I screened the film in Los Angeles. I thoughtfully wrote my questions on the little pads of paper placed in my room at the Century Plaza hotel. I laid out my best interview outfit—black pants from Ann Taylor and a fitted, charcoal-gray sweater from Banana Republic. I wore my finest jewelry given to me by my parents. I took extra time to do my hair and makeup. And I reviewed my questions over and over again. After a couple hours of pre-interview preparation in my hotel room, I headed out the door to tackle the interviews for my first movie junket.

When I checked in for my interviews, a representative from the movie studio sent me to a large room set up as a holding suite for all reporters. I walked into the room and didn't know a soul. I was definitely intimidated. And honestly, I felt like I was way out of my league. All of the reporters seemed to know each another. They were laughing and joking over sodas and snacks and didn't seem interested in including a new stranger from Cleveland, Ohio. There were reporters in the room from some of the big shows like *Entertainment Tonight* and *E! News*. These were people I watched on TV! I couldn't believe I was in the same room with them.

My heart started to race with insecurity, and I heard my inner voice say, "What the heck are you doing here? You don't belong with this crowd." But I couldn't turn back now. I had a job to do and a personal goal to meet. I wanted to be a reporter, and this was my opportunity.

I timidly took my place on an empty chair in the corner of the room. I didn't speak to anyone. I stayed focused, looked at my notes, and rehearsed my questions in my head. My goal was to do my interviews without looking at my note pad. I knew that I would keep my notes in my lap for security, just in case I forgot a question or felt lost at some point in the interview. But I also wanted to seem prepared and natural. While I was going through my quiet preparation, I heard someone call my name. It was a girl wearing headphones. She seemed very official. This was it. I was being called to begin my interviews with the cast of *The Insider*.

The first actress I interviewed was Gina Gershon. The only thing I remember about the interview was that Gina had really full lips, and her makeup artist kept applying shiny lip gloss throughout the interview. I remember complimenting Gina on the color of her lip gloss and secretly wished I had the same color on my lips. I thought that her shiny lip gloss might make me look more glamorous too. I was just wearing a boring matte lipstick that didn't have glamour power. But I needed to stay focused on being a good reporter. And the glossiness of my lipstick had no impact on good Q&A. The interview was a quick four minutes. That was all the time the movie studio allowed for junket interviews. The interview with Gina seemed to go well. She was nice, and I got through all of my questions with no big mistakes. My next interview was Christopher Plummer.

Christopher Plummer was the only actor on my interview list that day with credits that were familiar to me. Mr. Plummer is Hollywood royalty. He was Captain Von Trapp, for crying out loud! But it wasn't his famous role in *The Sound of Music* that got me excited to meet him. It was his role as William Fawcett Robinson in the movie *Somewhere in Time*. I was a little girl the first time I saw Jane Seymour play the character of Elise McKenna in *Somewhere in Time*. I remember sitting in the cozy family room of my parents' house, wearing a long white nightgown with tiny yellow flowers and a matching cotton robe. I wished that one day I might be like fictitious stage actress Elise McKenna. And now, over a decade later, the man sitting across from me was my closest connection to that movie. (On a side note, I did interview Jane Seymour years later. She read my favorite passage from *Somewhere in Time*. It was a magical moment for me, and Jane was lovely in every way.)

Of course I had to ask Christopher Plummer about one of my favorite films now that he was sitting in front of me. I hoped he loved the movie just as much as I did. After I asked a few questions about his current film, I moved on to my selfish question. I even recall the joy in my voice when I asked him about the film that I owned on DVD and would watch alone in my apartment on some idle Saturday night. And as I anticipated his joyful response, there was a pause. And then he answered. The answer was brief. It definitely was not joyful. In fact, I got the feeling that he didn't like my favorite film at all. My recollection of his lack of enthusiasm for *Somewhere in Time* was a total letdown. But I moved along and finished the interview with questions about the current movie he was promoting. Overall I came out of that interview unscathed. Just disappointed that Christopher Plummer and I didn't bond over a love story about a man who travels through time to meet the woman of his dreams in *Somewhere in Time*. But that's okay. I still love the way Mr. Plummer sings "Edelweiss."

Up next, the leading man, Russell Crowe. The actor I never heard of until this work assignment. And according to the articles I read, he was not the warm and fuzzy type. But he was the reason I was in LA. He was the reason why our show's entertainment reporter passed on doing this movie junket. I took that reporter's place. And suddenly this moment felt like a huge life moment for me.

I walked into the interview suite where Russell Crowe was sitting. He didn't look anything like the middle-aged man he played in the movie. Sitting before me was a young man with rugged good looks. His hair was a little longer and messy on top. He had some facial hair and was casually dressed. I introduced myself with a handshake. His grip was firm. He smiled and his eyes were friendly. I thought, "So far so good."

After our initial introduction, the next words I chose to speak were, "You clean up nice." *What???* Why did I just say that? It was my voice, so I had to take ownership of the words. But I had never met Russell Crowe before this moment. I had no idea what he typically looked like before or after a shower!

I quickly hoped that I hadn't insulted him. The last thing I wanted was to make my first impression that of a young, stupid reporter. But he laughed and thanked me. And then, in his wonderful Australian accent, Russell Crowe asked me how long I had been a reporter in Cleveland. I told him that I was not a reporter but an associate producer filling in for our show's entertainment reporter.

I recall that he cocked his head back with a quizzical look and said, "You're not in front of the camera?"

I thought, "Uh-oh, what does this mean? Is he mad that a producer is interviewing him and not a reporter?" But I was honest. I told him that I did not appear on camera.

He then asked me a second question in a sincere tone, "Do you want to be a reporter?"

In this moment, I had a conversation in my head. It was a conversation that lasted about a millisecond because I had to respond to Russell's question. I was trying to decide if he was pleased or displeased that a producer, not an on-air reporter, was in the room interviewing him. And I also wondered why he was asking *me* questions when the interview was supposed to be about *him*. I decided in my mind that Russell's question, based on his tone, was a good thing.

I responded, "Yes, I do want to be a reporter. It's something I'm working on."

Russell continued his line of questioning by asking, "What is your boss's name?"

I gave him the name of the general manager of my television station. This was the person in charge of all big decisions at work. And this particular general manager was about to get a message from Russell Crowe. The actor thought for a moment. And then looking at the camera in front of him, he said, "This is a message for [general manager]. This is Russell Crowe in Los Angeles from the film *The Insider*. If you don't put this woman on the air, you need to get yourself a pair of glasses, mate."

The entire time Russell Crowe spoke, I grinned from ear to ear. And when he finished his message for my station manager in Cleveland, I loudly replied, "I love you, and I will see every movie you ever make!"

In that exact moment Russell Crowe gained my loyalty with his words. And it wasn't even a scripted moment. I was a young girl on her first interview assignment. I sat in that room a rookie from the Midwest with hopes and dreams of becoming a television reporter. An established reporter with whom I worked had passed on interviewing Russell Crowe, which gave me the opportunity to meet and talk to him. Later that year, Russell Crowe received an Oscar nomination for best actor for his role in *The Insider*. The following year he won the Academy Award for best actor in *The Gladiator*. Today Russell Crowe is a household name. And on my first "reporting assignment," I got a recorded endorsement from Academy Award winner Russell Crowe!

My interview with Russell that day was just okay, to be perfectly honest. I didn't ask the most thought-provoking questions. But I blame that on my youth and inexperience. I did, however, learn three very important lessons that day. They are lessons that I remind myself of frequently. And they are lessons I will pass on to you, even though it's highly unlikely that you will ever interview Russell Crowe. But the lessons are universal no matter how old you are, how much money you make, where you live, or your type of employment. The first lesson came from the entertainment reporter who passed on interviewing Russell Crowe. That reporter really missed out on meeting an interesting person. The reporter's missed opportunity became my great opportunity. Through this encounter, I learned that everyone has a story if you take the time to listen. And just because a person is not popular, the most influential person in the room or an A-list actor doesn't mean that he or she is not interesting. Enjoy meeting new people and take time to talk to them. You never know what might come from that conversation. Conversations are a great way to network. And good conversations teach you how to listen and be inquisitive. Be interested in the people with whom you are talking. It will make you more interesting to them.

The second lesson I learned that day seems like an obvious one. But I think it's worth reminding you to always say yes to new opportunities, even if you're scared or think they may be a waste of time. I was nervous to leave the comfort of my Midwest broadcast surroundings and fly to the West Coast to interview Hollywood actors for the first time. And I felt more panicked when I was surrounded by the best of the best in broadcasting. Sometimes you may question whether or not you're good enough when you're presented with a new challenge. When you question yourself, it's based on fear. And it's usually your fear of failure. But I say sprint forward and kick fear's ass! Sure, you may fail. But failure is better than never trying at all. New opportunities often open the door for better opportunities. Look for opportunities, no matter how big or small. When you chase an opportunity, you will always be moving forward.

And finally, my third and valuable life lesson came from meeting Russell Crowe. I learned that you should not judge people by what is heard, read, or said about them. This is very important to remember. You should only judge people by the way they treat you and your loved ones. I half expected Russell Crowe to be an asshole when I met him. I was wrong. He was the complete opposite. And to this day, he's one of my favorite people that I've ever interviewed. People can surprise you. So hold your preconceived judgments.

Years later, I interviewed Russell Crowe again. I told him what he did for me a decade before. After thousands of interviews, I knew Russell wouldn't remember me or his brief recording to promote my career. But he kissed me on the cheek, hugged me, and humbly thanked me for reminding him. My opinion of Russell Crowe has not changed. I still think he's fantastic and one of the most gifted actors of our time.

That moment was a Hollywood dream for me. But that moment also ignited a fire within me. My desire to be a television reporter was stronger than ever. A Hollywood actor's words encouraged me to chase my dream. I didn't want to just be on television. I wanted to be good. I wanted to be successful. I wanted to continue doing movie junkets and become an entertainment reporter. Even if superstardom wasn't in my cards, I had a goal. And the goal was to do big things, starting with my television career.

I felt I had proved something to myself on my first travel assignment. I proved that I could walk into a job, surrounded by people more accomplished than me, and get the job done with a smile on my face and confidence in my voice. If I was able to replay the interviews I did that day, I know I would see a young girl who needed to perfect her interviewing skills. But I walked into a room feeling insecure while keeping my head up and getting the job done. I was proud of myself. My work that day led to another assignment. The following weekend I flew back to Los Angeles to interview Academy Award winner Tom Hanks. My opportunities kept getting better! I was moving forward.

Being entrusted with the Tom Hanks interview was thrilling for me! I wasn't an actual reporter yet, and Tom was one of the most famous actors in the world. He was also known to be one of the nicest guys in the business, with a fondness for my hometown of Cleveland. This interview, I thought, would be a breeze. But the closer I got to my interview date, the more nervous I became. I couldn't believe I was going to interview Oscar winner Tom Hanks! This was going to be one of the best memories of my life. I was determined to make this a flawless interview!

There were so many thoughts racing through my brain during the days that led up to my interview with Tom Hanks:

Would this interview be career changing for me? Would I do a good job? Would Tom automatically be nice to me because I was from Cleveland and he liked my hometown? Could I pull off this interview and sound like a pro?

I was about to find out. My Tom Hanks interview day arrived. As hours counted down to minutes, I felt my palms start to get sweaty. While I was sitting outside Tom's interview room, I remember fanning myself with a stack of papers because I was so hot. It was a nervous hot, not a room temperature hot. And then I was called upon to begin my interview. I walked into the room and shook Tom's hand. But before I shook his hand, I wiped my own hand on my pants to dry off my sweaty palms.

I started the interview. My voice sounded playful, my questions were fun and Tom was laughing and answering everything perfectly. But while he was talking, I was having a conversation in my head. It went something like this:

Oh my God, I can't believe I'm sitting across from Tom Hanks. The interview is going well, but my hands are still sweaty. And now I think my upper lip is starting to sweat. Oh no, there might be some sweat coming down the side of my face! I wonder if Tom can see my sweat beads. Wow, these lights are bright! I think the lights are making it really hot in here. Why isn't Tom sweating? Dear God, please let this interview end before I'm completely soaked! This is so embarrassing. Should I wrap up the interview early? No, I have to use all of the time the movie studio is giving me or they'll never ask me back. I look like a rookie. I wonder if Tom Hanks thinks I'm a superfan rather than a journalist? Should I wipe my sweaty hands one more time on my pants or will that be obvious? Tom is probably so grossed out by my sweat. He might want to wash his hands if I say good-bye with a handshake. PLEASE just let this interview be over now!!!

The interview ended. I did shake Tom's hand. And I asked someone else if the room seemed hot or was it just me? My interview with Tom aired on our show in Cleveland, but luckily the shots of me were cut out because I looked like a sweaty mess! Years later, I interviewed Tom Hanks again. I didn't remind him of the sweaty palm incident. And thank goodness this time my hands were dry. Mentally I had redeemed myself.

The more celebrity interviews I did, the more confident I became. Eventually I felt I found my niche. Even though California was a long trip from Cleveland, I loved traveling to the West Coast. The repetition of celebrity interviews helped me to be a better interviewer and develop a rapport with the people I was interviewing. Plus, it gave me a chance to gauge the skills of other reporters in my field who worked all over the country. It's always a motivator to work with people who challenge you to improve your skills. The movie junkets gave me confidence in my abilities. And they gave me an opportunity to perfect my interviewing skills. My Grandma Mary was right. This was the profession for me.

Maybe you've always known what you wanted to do for a living. Some people are just lucky to know their career path early on. They have their chosen profession mapped out, whether it's a doctor, an architect, an actor, a makeup artist, or a teacher. Maybe you're someone who is often redefining yourself. Some people start off in one profession in their twenties and then reroute themselves in their forties. It's easy to do something safe and comfortable, but much more thrilling to find your passion and follow that dream. I once asked a professional life coach if you need to have passion in your career to be successful. She told me no and that there are many people who are extremely successful in their profession who don't have passion for their work. But we both agreed that passion for your work is not a profession but a calling.

So how do you find your calling in life? And can that calling change? Yes, of course it can change. We are all born to do more than one thing in life. But while you're searching for your calling, your next chapter, or your first start, ask yourself...What are your strengths? What gifts do people recognize in you? What brings you joy and excitement? What fuels your desire to learn more? At what times do you shine the brightest? As you answer these questions, perhaps the answers will remind you of your latent passions.

I had the dream to be a television reporter. I took advantage of early opportunities that came my way, and those opportunities turned my dream into my reality. My career path started big, with A-list celebrity interviews. This occurred due to a combination of luck, good timing, proving that I had the ability to get the job done, and believing in my dream. Believe in yourself and your abilities, even when others do not. There is truth in the theory of positive thinking. If you believe in your future, it's much more likely to become a reality than if you keep telling yourself it won't happen. When a baseball player is in a slump, he's more likely to keep striking out if he fears his talent is gone. But if you can be like Babe Ruth and point to the direction of your home run, you're more likely to hit it out of the park. And remember this: Opportunities don't happen when you sit on your couch and just wish for them. Go after it! Run toward great opportunities. Even if the opportunities scare you. Discover what you were born to do. And have passion for your work. Listen to the music that motivates you and live your playlist.

two

It's Not the Critic Who Counts

Playlist Song & Artist: "Perfect" Alanis Morissette

I'm not sure where my desire to be perfect came from. I was never the smartest kid in my class, and my parents didn't scold me for not getting straight As. I was never the most athletic or fastest on the swim team. But my mom and dad were always there to cheer me on at every event and seemed proud of me even if I lost. I suppose they were proud of the fact that I finished the race while trying my hardest. I wasn't the prettiest, the most popular, the most talented, or the most anything. Although I did get the award for "Most Creative" in eighth grade at St. Jude Elementary in the small town of Elyria, Ohio. The point is, even though I wasn't considered "the best" by society's standards, my parents always made me feel I was terrific. So maybe my desire to be perfect comes from the fact that I'm a Virgo and supposedly we're perfectionists? Or maybe it's self-imposed perfectionism? Nonetheless, this idea of being perfect all the time became an issue for me. Especially when my flaws were displayed on live television.

When you're just getting started in your career, it's true that you typically start from the bottom and work your way up, no matter your chosen profession. I went from working as an associate producer in Cleveland to taking my first reporting job in Zanesville, Ohio. Zanesville is located in Appalachian Ohio. It sits close to the West Virginia border. In television, market sizes are ranked from largest to smallest, with number one being the largest. New York and Los Angeles, for example, are usually ranked number one and number two. Zanesville was market number 203 when I was hired as a reporter. That's 203 on a list that went from 1 to 210.

My first news reporting job wasn't glamorous, but it was the start I needed to pursue a bigger dream. A news director once told me that it didn't matter if I got my first on-air break in San Francisco, California, or Mobile, Alabama. He said I just needed someone to give me a chance. I believe that's true in any profession. Get your foot in the door. And then either work hard to be promoted within the company or get your foot out the door and into another one where you can advance.

My first on-air job was like going back to grade school. I learned the basics, such as how to sniff out a good story, how to write a news story quickly (sometimes in less than five minutes to get it on the air on time for a newscast), and how to ask the right questions in an interview. I also learned from my mistakes. Beginning with something as trivial as what color of clothing didn't look good on TV to something more important, such as what to do when I put the wrong information on the air. I also learned what it felt like to receive viewer criticism. It was an ugly part of the business that would follow me throughout my career. I made plenty of mistakes on the air in the small town of Zanesville. And the viewers let me know when I made mistakes. It was typical to have a morning meeting with the news director and fellow reporters to discuss plans for the day and review the newscast from the night before. During one particular meeting,

I recall the news director playing a voice message for the group to hear. It was a local viewer complaining about a mistake that I made on the air. It was slightly embarrassing to be used as an example in front of my colleagues. But our news director went on to say that it was a mistake that anyone could have made. He wanted us to be mindful of our storytelling. He was right. And so was the viewer. I was learning simple and important skills every day.

Over time, with repetition and practice, I became comfortable with my on-camera skills. Financially I wasn't commanding a high paycheck. I signed a contract for $21,000 a year. And I knew some of the other reporters had second jobs just to pay their rent. My rent was around $400 a month. And my three-room apartment looked pretty empty. I had a bed, a dresser for my clothes, a couple of lamps, and two end tables. I'm not sure why I had the end tables because I never had a couch. My bed was the place where I ate, watched TV, and slept. My bed was a full-sized mattress with a metal bed frame. Nothing fancy or particularly comfortable.

I was typically assigned four to five stories a day when I worked in Zanesville. It was rare that I covered hard-hitting news. Although an occasional murder story would unfold that gave all of the young journalists in town a chance to put our skills to the test. After seven months of reporting in Zanesville, I longed for a bigger city and a better job. I made the decision to leave my first reporting job in market number 203 and take a producing job in Cleveland, market number seventeen. On a beautiful fall day in October, my dad drove south on I-77 to Zanesville in a U-Haul and helped me pack up my things. I moved back to Cleveland, hired to be a television producer, with the hope of getting back on the air. It was a risky move for a young woman who was pursuing an on-air career. I was taking myself off of the air to go behind the camera while betting on a chance to land an on-air job in Cleveland. When you're making a career decision, you may be faced with the choice to make a lateral move, take a pay cut, or take a lower position. And none of those options seem ideal. But sometimes you have a feeling in your gut that it's the right move to make even if it doesn't look like you're advancing on paper. I felt that my move back to Cleveland would lead to something better. One step back might lead to three steps forward. It turned out to be a great move for me.

After years of low wages, entry-level positions, grunt work, thankless hours, and time in a small market, I still loved television. Especially live television. There was something exciting about the pressure of having to execute my job perfectly, yet knowing how to handle it gracefully when I made a mistake. There is an element of surprise in live television. You never know what someone is going to say or do until it happens. And you need to be alert and ready to respond in that moment. With live television, you can have a plan, but that plan can change in an instant because of breaking news, technical difficulties, or some other unexpected reason. All of these scenarios might cause fear and panic in some people, but they excited me. They got my adrenaline going. Even though I was not working in front of the camera, I was still working in an environment that excited me. I held that job as a producer for the next six years. And I began to wonder if I would ever make it back on the air as a reporter. And then one day, an unexpected opportunity presented itself.

The station where I worked had plans to start an hour-long live weekly talk show. It was to be called *Good Company*. I knew that I was going to be the producer of this show with a chance to contribute some celebrity interviews. I was pretty low on the food chain at the television station and never thought that I would be considered to host this new show. But even with that thought in mind, I knew that I had to go after the position. Yes, I had faced rejection in the past, and I didn't want to be met with rejection again. Yes, I was still underqualified if you looked at my resume. But I knew in my heart that I would be great at the job if I was given the chance. And there was no way that anyone was going to give me the position if I didn't ask for it. So I asked. I ignored the critic in my head and the critics of the past. I took a leap of faith and pitched myself as the host of the new show. Convincing the decision makers wasn't easy. But in the end, I got the job. Belief. Courage. Guts. Perseverance. Intelligence. These are all ingredients for winners. And I wanted to be a winner.

I started hosting the new show that fall of 2005. There were four hosts on the show. Two women and two men. I was the youngest of the foursome. There were changes made to the show until the last moment before we went on the air for the first time. Traces of chaos were everywhere. Set designers were still pounding nails into the show's set moments before our first live broadcast. Producers were running around with stacks of papers in their hands while having frantic conversations on their cell phones. And interns were taking care of guests and making sure that they were comfortable. It was cold in the studio, even under all of the bright lights. The set was styled to look like a cozy living room. The backdrop was blue, and the couches were a shade of neutral. There were large fake plants on the set. They looked kind of tacky, but faux plants are often a typical accessory on local talk shows. The studio was busy and the energy was exciting!

I did everything I could to prepare myself for my first show. I had my makeup done by one of the best makeup artists in town. I got a fresh haircut and bought all of the right styling products to make my hair camera ready. I aligned myself with a local retailer so that I had a new outfit to wear every day. And I wrote all of my interviews so that I sounded in control of my thoughts and questions. I was nervous, but I did everything I could to make sure I was perfect. The floor director, who keeps everything running smoothly in the studio, told us to take our seats and pointed to the camera as we were about to go live. Five...four...three...two...one...It was show time!

I put on my best smile and remember feeling anxious and excited as the show started. *Good Company* had its own jingle that played while an animated graphic rolled to introduce the new show. As soon as the red light above the studio camera lit up, I knew we were live. The format of the show allowed the hosts to begin by chatting with each other and to our viewers about our lives and discuss some relevant topics of the day. I knew quickly that the first show wasn't going well. As hosts, we were stepping all over each other. It appeared that there was no chemistry. We were off to a messy start. It was definitely not perfect. And it was live for everyone to see. In all fairness, the first broadcast of any show is rarely the best show. There is typically a nervous energy, and it often takes time for a television team to get into a groove. It took us time, but eventually we found our rhythm and developed chemistry with each other.

As a foursome, we seemed to be randomly paired together for the show. But I always felt that we genuinely liked each other. This can be rare in television. Often someone's ego gets in the way. But we all seemed to have our egos in check. At the head of the group was an older gentleman who was a local icon in town. After spending many decades in front of the camera, he laughingly referred to himself as an "old geezer" now that he was in his late seventies. He was a man of a million ties. And most of his ties had some kind of food printed on them, as he was a true foodie and cookbook author. This veteran host brought a sense of history, knowledge, and an ease to the show. Of the four hosts, he was the most well known in town. He was kind, smart, gracious, and one of the best people I've ever worked with in my career. I first met him when I did an internship in my late teens. Eventually I worked alongside him as a producer. Now that I was nearing thirty, I felt at ease sitting next to a man I had known for most of my career. The other female on the show was a former meteorologist in town. She was in her forties and had blond hair, blue eyes, and a wicked sense of humor. Well known for her years of delivering the weather, she was funny, ditzy, and likable. Whatever came out of her mouth was unpredictable, and there was something frustratingly refreshing about a woman in television who would show up with coffee stains on her suit and dog hair all over her clothes. She didn't care what other people thought of her. It was a lesson that took years for me to learn.

I still remember the first time I received "hate mail" from a viewer of our show. I told my female cohost about the nasty words that an anonymous person wrote to me. I'm sure she could hear the sound of defeat in my voice as I sadly read the mean e-mail. She told me, "Delete, delete, delete." Her message to me was that I should erase the e-mail and not pay attention to the mean-spirited critics of the world. She was right. But that advice is easier said than done.

The second male host on the show had been a friend of mine before the show started. He was a product of reality television with no other background in broadcast television. Well known in town by his peers as a club promoter, he was tall, dark, and handsome. And he often boasted about doing five hundred abdominal crunches a day because he was focused on staying in good shape. He always wore well-tailored suits but made his appearance more casual by going tieless. He was the type of guy who seemed to embrace making fun of himself, and as a result, he was somewhat of a class clown on the show. When the producers were looking to cast a second male on the show, I had recommended him. I thought he had the looks and personality that we wanted for the open spot. It was quickly decided that he won the job.

And then there was me. I was a tall, slender, Italian brunette with olive skin, green eyes, and a long nose that reflected the small traces of my Slovac heritage. I was twenty-nine years old when the show first started. And at that time, I was the least known to viewers. I had a lot of experience working behind the camera in television, but this was my first big introduction to the local audience. I was fairly well connected in the entertainment industry, and the producers wanted to add an entertainment element to our show. I also think my boss was hoping that I would appeal to the coveted demographic, women ages eighteen to forty-nine. So with my stylish outfits and lively personality, I hoped to win everyone over by just being myself. My new position as a talk show host was a dream come true for me. Especially in my hometown, where most of my family lived. And at the time, my Grandma Mary was still alive. She made the first prediction that I should be on TV. It was special for me that she was able to watch me every day.

Our show was never a perfect show. It always had its flaws. But I loved my job. The opportunity to write thoughtful interviews and engage in conversations with interesting, funny, and entertaining guests fueled my excitement to go to work every day. It also felt wonderful to have a vehicle to help philanthropic people spread the word about their positive causes. Plus, I got to travel the globe and meet people I admired, like Meryl Streep, Anthony Hopkins, and Robert De Niro. I was living an exciting life! Much of what I did during the years of hosting my first talk show was more than I ever imagined. I appeared on the covers of local magazines like *Westshore Magazine* and *Cleveland Magazine*, which was the most circulated magazine in town (and I think my parents bought every issue when I was on the cover). I flew to Bora Bora with Vince Vaughn (I can say that because he was on my plane). I had Hollywood actors ask for my phone number (and I pretended to feel special even though I knew I was one of many women being asked). I got to film a scene in the blockbuster movie *The Avengers* and was paid for my role (even though my part was cut to a nanosecond). And I had a guest-starring role in the Broadway musical *Chicago* (for one night only). Some of these moments were grand in scale and others were trivial. But I was making the most of my young and single life! I had many blessings. But those blessings came with a reality. The reality was my professional life was fun, but it was definitely not perfect.

I'm not a celebrity. George Clooney is a celebrity. Oprah is a celebrity. Justin Timberlake is a celebrity. And LeBron James is a celebrity. I was just a Cleveland talk show host, which made me a local celebrity in my hometown. And I always joked that I was only a "celebrity" in my parents' eyes. I just happened to have a job where more than a few people around town recognized me. And believe me, there were plenty of people who didn't know who the heck I was. Something strange happens when you're in the public eye, even on a small scale. People feel that they can say anything to you and about you. Especially when it comes to negative comments. Those comments typically present themselves in the form of hate mail. And hate mail almost always comes from anonymous writers. In the television industry, my colleagues and I would simply refer to these people as "haters." I received e-mails saying that I was ugly, fat, and stupid. One person told me that he couldn't stand the sound of my voice and another said that no matter how many times I wore black, I couldn't hide my chunky arms. And some people would drop me a note to tell me that I was the worst part of the show. The haters didn't come close to outnumbering the sweet and thoughtful messages I got from good-hearted people. But the criticisms were harder for me to forget. I'm human. Their mean words got to me.

When these cruel comments were sent to me, I started wondering to myself...Did I need to lose weight? Did that dress make me look fat? Should I do something new with my hair? Was my voice really that bad? Was I asking good questions during my interviews? Was I even good at what I did?

When others criticize us, it sets off a trigger that makes us doubt ourselves. We make the mistake of allowing other people's words and thoughts to become real. This is a choice we make. We can choose to believe what others say about us. Or we can choose to believe what we know is true about ourselves.

The negative comments directed at me were challenging my desire to be perfect. As I reflected on the hateful words written by strangers, I knew my self-esteem was being tested. I needed to put that negativity into perspective. First, I had to accept the obvious. These digs were written anonymously, which is cowardly. It's very doubtful that any of these people would have the guts to make the same mean-spirited comments to my face. I needed to dismiss the critics' words and place no value on their statements. I also had to assume that the people attacking my appearance didn't look like supermodel Heidi Klum. Have you ever noticed that the people who tear others down usually look ugly from the inside out? Hate can change your appearance. And not for the better. When people attack you, your instinct is to attack back or defend yourself. I did both when I first received hate mail. I recall many times trying to win someone over by acting out the cliché of killing them with kindness. Sometimes I lost sleep over people's hurtful words. But as the years passed, I learned something valuable. I learned that it's a waste of energy to let a nameless, faceless person make you feel bad about yourself. Haters are usually very unhappy people. And I can guarantee that they don't lose sleep over the people they attack. When someone attacks you with negative comments, seek out people in your life who care about you. Let the people who love you reinforce your self-worth. And their assessment of you will be much more accurate than the people who are just plain mean. The opinions of people who are important in your life matter abundantly more than the opinions of people who anonymously or secretly try to hurt you.

Learning to ignore criticism is something I still work on. But I believe that practicing it, and ultimately mastering it, leads to better mental health. Some of the most powerful and influential people in the world are criticized on a daily basis. But it doesn't stop them from moving forward with their goals. Take any president of the United States, for example. There's always a good chance that a large percentage of people don't like the president and don't agree with all of the president's decisions. But the president is still the leader of the free world. It's the most important job in our country and arguably the world. Presidents are flawed and certainly not perfect. And they are highly criticized. But if they allowed every criticism to define them, they wouldn't be very effective at their job.

In a speech given by President Theodore Roosevelt in France on April 23, 1910, often referred to as "The Man in the Arena" speech, one notable passage begins with the words, *"It is not the critic who counts; not the man who points out how the strong man stumbles, or where the doer of deeds could have done them better. The credit belongs to the man who is actually in the arena."* President Roosevelt's speech continues with profound words of wisdom. The overall message is that credit should not be given to those who criticize but to those who do the hard work. Roosevelt goes on to deliver the idea that even if you fail at your work, at least you failed while putting all of your passion and effort into something that you care about. I keep a copy of this passage with me and make a point to read it on a regular basis. The criticisms I received while I was on television were usually about something superficial, like the size of my nose or an outfit that I wore. But sometimes my skills were criticized. I welcomed thoughtful feedback, even if it wasn't positive. But when the feedback was mean and hurtful, I reminded myself that it's not the critic who counts. The opinions of mean people hold no real value.

Over time, my confidence became stronger and so did my popularity on the show. As my popularity increased, so did my sense of importance. Not in the sense that I became an egomaniac. In fact, I lean more toward modest than overly confident. But there were days when I felt invincible and on top of the world. And then, just as I starting getting too comfortable with my television self, I was reminded that I had flaws. Usually through my own mistakes. Mistakes can be a good thing. They force us to examine our personal weaknesses and work on them. And that's exactly what I had to do after a live interview that went terribly wrong with a fairly well-known comedian.

Every week, my show featured a comedian performing at one of the local comedy clubs. Usually the scheduled comedian was just flying into town from Los Angeles on the red eye. The hours of a morning show are not conducive to the working hours of a late-night comedian. So understandably, because of jet lag and sleep schedules, not every comedian was ready to perform with high energy at ten o'clock in the morning. One morning we had comedian Rob Schneider on the show. Rob was best known for his roles on *Saturday Night Live*, the *Deuce Bigalow* movies, and appearing in Adam Sandler films. I can't recall if Rob flew in on the red eye that morning, but I do remember that we were off to a rocky start the moment the interview started.

When I introduced him, I said something like, "Joining us this morning is comedian Rob Schneider, who recently starred in the movie *Grown Ups*." While that sounds like a perfectly natural introduction, there was a problem with my statement. It was incorrect. I mentioned the name of the film *Grown Ups* as though it was already released. The problem was that the film had not come out in theaters yet. Rob corrected me immediately.

I apologized for verbally prereleasing his film and tried to move on with the interview. But it seemed that my guest did not want to let me off the hook. Rob incessantly brought up my spoken mistake throughout our interview. I remember that at one point it became so uncomfortable that my cohost had to tell Rob to back off. I felt that Rob was tough on me and seemed relentless about my mistake. But I made a bigger professional and personal mistake during this interview. As the interview progressed, I might as well have folded my arms and pouted in protest of this guest. I had mentally checked out. A few minutes into the interview, after Rob verbally disciplined me on the air for what felt like the hundredth time, I stopped asking questions and let my cohost continue on his own with the interview. I was physically present but not participating. I remember thinking that I couldn't believe this guy was on *my show* and treating me like an idiot. I didn't think that I deserved that kind of treatment for one misspoken error. And even though I thought he acted like a huge ass, I was acting worse.

I recall that my entire team agreed that Rob Schneider was not nice that day. But I gave a wrong fact on the air. And I stopped doing my job because my ego was bruised. Even though I thought this guest took his relentless scolding a little too far, my facts should have been correct. After the show, I told the producers that I never wanted Rob Schneider back on our set because of the way he treated me. I had an attitude. And I anointed myself as the "God of Guests Cast off the Show." But my attitude was foolish. Was he the best guest ever? Absolutely not. But I made two mistakes that day. The first was human error and certainly forgivable. The second was a mistake of choice. And a bad one. It was unprofessional of me to shut down during the interview. And it needed to be the first and the last time that I ever made that decision. My job as the interviewer was to keep things moving along, no matter how uncomfortable it got. I know that while I was publicly blaming the guest for being a jerk, I was privately angrier with myself for being wrong. I had to accept the reality that I was going to make mistakes of human error. It was time to make peace with the fact that I couldn't be perfect every day.

But some flaws are worth self-reflection. It's hard to look at ourselves and recognize our personality flaws. I think it's unfortunate that we are so quick to point out our physical flaws but don't try to look beneath the surface when we look in the mirror. It's important to examine our entire makeup to improve as human beings. Maybe you have a tendency to be conde-scending, judgmental, gossipy, selfish, impatient, a know-it-all, or have issues with anger. Whatever your personality flaw, ask yourself...Why am I this way? How can I improve?

My flaw in the Rob Schneider example was that I was suf-fering from a case of entitlement and stubbornness. I acted entitled because I demanded respect from someone who didn't know me. And I was stubborn because I stopped doing my job once my ego was damaged. I owed my cohost, the producers, and maybe even Rob Schneider an apology for stubbornly shut-ting down during that interview. And internally, I was hardest on myself. I was mad at myself for messing up that interview. It's easy to say the words "I'm not perfect." But it's harder to accept the fact that our imperfections aren't always likable traits.

Know this to be true. No one is perfect. Don't search for the perfect man, woman, job, or material possession. Everything has its flaws. If you seek what is flawless, you will search for a very long time. And likely never find what you're looking for.

When I began the journey of living my playlist, I noticed something special about imperfection. One day I decided to take a walk in the rain. It was the kind of day when I would normally dread being caught outside. A day when sweat pants, a good John Hughes movie, and a bag of potato chips on a comfy couch would be preferred to walking in the rain. But this day turned out to be one of my favorite walks. I became aware of beautiful imperfections. Every tree was a different size and shape. And sometimes the tree bark was peeling off. None of the leaves from the trees had the same pattern. And some had holes in them. I looked at the neighbor's perfectly manicured lawns, but noticed that some parts had brown spots. It was a day when the sun was hidden by dark clouds, which allowed my eyes to observe the scenery without squinting. The trees stood tall and strong. The air smelled clean and fresh. And the feel of each raindrop on my face became refreshing. I didn't care that my clothes were wet or that my hair was a mess. When we look to nature, we see beauty. We see perfection. We don't notice the flaws. Or we don't define them as such. It was a seemingly flawed day, but it felt almost perfect. I embraced the imperfection of the day. And it was glorious!

three

Mirror Mirror on the Wall

Playlist Song & Artist: "Shake It Out" Florence and the Machine

Shake it out. It's a phrase my friend in Major League Baseball told me that professional players use during a game. Especially pitchers when they're on the mound and struggling to get through an inning. Someone, usually the coach, walks up to the mound and tells the pitcher to shake it out. And then the coach tells that pitcher to go after it and win the game. The role of a coach is one of the most important roles that a person can play in someone's life. And with that role comes much responsibility. The responsibility to teach, grow, nurture, guide, strengthen, and support. For most of us, unless we become lifelong athletes, the role of a coach is that of a mentor. As soon as I heard the song *Shake It Out* by Florence and the Machine, I added it to my playlist. I was going through a difficult time in my professional life because the mentor I had looked up to for a long time no longer seemed to support me. It became a painful experience for me. I found a female mentor in my twenties whom I trusted and admired. She told me that she wanted to help me grow my career. But eventually she broke me down. I discovered that my mentor wasn't rooting for me to win the game. And I didn't know how to shake her out. But this experience came with many lessons that I must pass on to others, especially women.

For the sake of this story, my mentor's name was Nestor Vance. But I just called her "NV" for short. NV had a personality like a hurricane. She came into a room with force and the ability to cause a lot of destruction. But sometimes there was a quiet before the storm, and you just had to sit and wait it out to see what her next move would be. I always knew when NV was about to enter a room because I could hear her loud voice coming from far away. There was a time when I welcomed that loud voice. Eventually I grew to fear it. NV had wavy hair, and her locks were the color of black coal. Her mane was often free flowing, but periodically she would pull it back away from her face. NV had blue eyes and fair skin that quickly changed to shades of pink and red when her emotions got the best of her, whether she was embarrassed, uncomfortable, or angry. Her skin color always showed her emotions. NV had a unique style that was her own. She showcased her flamboyant personality through her choice of fashion accessories. NV almost always wore a plain pantsuit. Her suits were typically a polyester material in a shade of navy or maroon. But she accessorized with artistic, colorful jewelry, like a parrot pin with feathers, a large fruit pendant, or a bracelet made of Sunkist bottle caps. And she often sported sneakers that were either silver or purple. Nothing ever matched, but that wasn't important to her. NV was several inches shorter than my five-foot-eight frame, but she was not afraid to be a space invader. NV came within an inch or two of me every time she spoke, which always felt like an unwelcome intrusion. NV laughed often, though I'm not sure what she was laughing about. It often seemed like an attention-seeking laugh. Most of the time it appeared as if she was laughing at herself. I think she viewed herself as a comedian. Maybe that was a career she secretly desired? But headlining the comedy circuit was never in her cards. NV always smelled of the same fragrance. It was a light scent, something floral but not offensive. Just a scent that was signature to her and left its mark every time she entered and exited a room. I think she was a woman who always wanted you to be aware of her presence.

I first met NV when I was in my early twenties and she was in her early forties. It was a brief exchange. I thought she was funny with a lot of energy. NV was also in the television industry. As my elder in the business, she was much more experienced. It became clear to me at that time that NV was a person of influence in the industry. And I was looking for someone to mentor me. She became that person.

In the beginning, I felt lucky to have NV as my mentor. And she often referred to me as her protégée. It was a label I was proud to wear because NV seemed to like having me under her wing. She invited me to parties attended by other people of influence in television. And she always introduced me as one of the bright female up-and-comers in the industry. NV's praise instilled bits of confidence in me. Sometimes NV would run an industry idea by me and ask for my thoughts. I couldn't believe she wanted my input! This made me feel important and smart.

In the beginning of my career, I found that some people wanted to attack my work. NV always seemed to defend me as if I was her younger sister. This made me feel loyalty toward her. And I completely trusted her. I felt so blessed to have the guidance of this woman as my mentor. And I believed that with her influence, NV would help nurture and develop my career.

After a couple years in my entry-level job, I had an opportunity to land a position that excited me and would further my career. I was nearing my late twenties, and it was time for me to take a step up in my profession. Of course my parents were excited and thought I would be perfect for the new position. My parents were always my biggest cheerleaders, along with NV. So I couldn't wait to tell her about this potential opportunity! I scheduled a lunch meeting with NV at a local restaurant to share the news. I was nervous about pursuing this new opportunity because I questioned whether or not I would get the job. I didn't want to face rejection. But when I imagined getting the job, I felt excited and empowered! I wanted NV's advice about this new position because of her success and influence in television.

As we dined over sandwiches and salads in the busy restaurant, I thoughtfully mapped out the reasons why I wanted this job. I explained why I thought I would excel in this new position. All the while, I figured I was preaching to the choir because I knew NV would support me. When she gave me her feedback, I was caught off guard. With a serious look on her face and certainty in her voice, I recall NV saying things like, "I don't know if your boss will give you that job." And "I don't think you're ready to handle that position." Her reaction confused me because it did not have the supportive tone I was expecting. Suddenly I felt like a small child whose parents just told her that she wasn't good enough to win first place. I had gone into our lunch feeling excited. And now I was deflated, which made me feel small and weak. I'm sure the look on my face showed my sense of disappointment and hurt, but NV didn't stop there. She went on to question my abilities. As I remember the conversation, NV told me that she didn't think I was good enough for the position. I was confused why my mentor wasn't building me up at a time when I had an opportunity to grow. I went into our lunch meeting feeling empowered. And now I was filled with self-doubt. When I left the restaurant, I felt a pit in my stomach. And when I got into my car, I hung my head and cried. What happened to my cheerleader? Going into that lunch, the voice inside my head told me that I could be anything that I wanted to be in life. And now my voice was telling me that I was not good enough. My confidence deflated the moment my mentor spoke her unsupportive words. Her comments were hurtful. NV's opinion mattered to me. And right now, it appeared her opinion of me was not good. I'll never forget how I felt in that moment. But I didn't let NV's discouraging words stop me. I pursued the job, and I got it.

My new job wasn't my first or last television opportunity, but it was certainly an exciting opportunity. This job gave me the chance to showcase my skills on live television. I felt confident that I was good at my job. And for the most part, I always received positive feedback from colleagues, viewers, and people in the community I met when I was out and about. One day during a lunch break, I drove to pick up NV for a visit. We planned to grab a quick drink at a local coffee shop. Even though NV had given me some disappointing feedback when I first talked to her about the job opportunity, I let it go because of her years of great mentoring and friendship. I was now established in my new role and felt comfortable with my talents. I never planned to ask NV's opinion of my work over this coffee date. I just wanted to catch up on our lives.

Apparently NV had a different idea. She had some things to say about my work and didn't hold back in sharing her opinions. Moments after I picked her up, NV launched into some rant about my delivery on television. I recall her criticizing the times that I shared personal stories about my life on TV. In so many words, I remember that NV told me that people didn't care about my personal stories and that I should stop pretending I was on *Regis and Kelly* because I was nothing like them. *Ouch!* That one stung. But I kept my eyes on the road and continued driving. I wanted to mute NV's loud voice, but she didn't quit. She went on to say that she had talked to some people around town about me and discovered that many people found me polarizing on the air. I couldn't believe that these words were coming out of her mouth. I thought we were getting together for iced teas and lattes. And now I wanted to make a pit stop at the local bar for a shot of Who-The-Hell-Are-You-And-What-Have-You-Done-With-My-Mentor? In five short minutes, NV told me that I was a Kelly Ripa poser and polarizing on TV! I was upset and speechless. How was I supposed to respond? I mumbled that I disagreed and changed the subject. But I was deflated before we even pulled into the coffee shop.

Up until this point, NV's hurtful comments always happened when we were together privately. In public, she continued to sing my praises and acted as if we were good friends. Of course this confused me, because one minute she was tearing me down and the other minute she was building me up. In hindsight, I see that this was clever manipulation. But over time NV became more reckless, or should I say more comfortable, in embarrassing me in front of other people. I was shocked when she chose to do this in front of a special woman in my life. That woman was my mother.

Before NV started manipulating my emotions, I often told my parents about the great female mentor I had found to help guide and advance me professionally. My parents were grateful that this established woman took a special interest in me. One day my mom stopped by my workplace to take me out to lunch. While we were out, we ran into NV. I was excited for NV and my mother to finally meet. My mom and I were dining at an upscale restaurant in town called Blue Point Grille, where white tablecloths are freshly starched and gourmet tea bags are presented in wooden tea boxes at the table. I happily waved my mentor over to meet my mom. I stood to greet her. When NV approached the table, she looked me up and down, and the first words out of her mouth were to tell me that I looked like a trollop. My eyes widened and my mouth dropped open as I looked down at the dress I was wearing. It was a designer black dress that hung about four inches above my knees. The back of my dress came midway down my back, but the front covered all

areas of my chest. The shoes I wore were three-inch black pat-
ent leather pumps. And my jewelry was silver and simple.

I've never used the word trollop to describe a woman, but if
you look it up in the dictionary, you'll see that it basically means
a slut. I've been described as many things in my life, some good,
some bad, but never a trollop or a slut. At least not to my knowledge. And NV said this in front of my mother! I was horrified.
And there were other people dining around us who could have
heard. My mom's face revealed how shocked and appalled she
was that this woman spoke those words publicly to her daughter. And I wouldn't be surprised if my mom was thinking...*This
is the woman you call your mentor?*

I was mad and embarrassed. Mad because I was not dressed
inappropriately. And even if I was, it was an inappropriate comment to make in front of my mother. I was embarrassed because
I had spoken so highly about this woman to my mom. NV's rude
comment was not one of high praise for me. I suppose I could
give her credit for saying those words to my face rather than
behind my back. But it was difficult to justify her belittling comment in that moment. Unfortunately, this wasn't the only time
that my female mentor embarrassed me in public. Her criticism
about my clothing was common. During the cold Cleveland
winters, I often wore UGG boots to keep my feet warm. One day
NV told me that she heard on the radio that UGG boots were
out of fashion. She then laughed a loud cackle and said that she
couldn't wait to tell me that I was wearing something that was
no longer considered stylish. I said nothing while I thought
about the lime-green high-top tennis shoes she was wearing
the last time we got together. NV's cutting comments continued
and became heightened once I reached professional success.

My job often required me to speak in front of large groups
of people. On this particular afternoon, I was giving a presentation to a group of women. I was well into my career and found
myself mentoring a few hopeful journalists. The topic of the

presentation was mentoring. I was speaking with ease and seemed to command everyone's attention. NV was in attendance and sitting in the back of the room. During the presentation I misspoke and had to correct myself. I believe I used the wrong word, acknowledged the mistake, and corrected it. It really wasn't a big deal. Just human error from talking for a long period of time. But without missing a beat, I remember that my supposed mentor (in a room full of women) yelled out, "And you call yourself an English major?" As if to imply that I wasn't smart because I misspoke. I saw the faces of the people in the room. They looked uncomfortable after this woman, my mentor, belittled me. I was publicly humiliated and embarrassed. I didn't know what to do or say, so I laughed it off and moved on with my presentation. But it was hard to refocus on the task at hand. I was just thrown a mean curve ball from the back of the room. And it was from someone I hoped was there to support me on the topic of mentoring. Why would *my* mentor do this in front of other people? Did it make her feel good to tear me down in front of others? Did she enjoy making me feel embarrassed? I was trying to appear confident as my speech continued, but inside I felt insecure because NV had drawn negative attention to my mistake in front of a large group of people.

On my drive home from the presentation, I was fixated on what had just happened. And I continued to stew over it all night and into the morning. If this woman I called my mentor was making fun of me publicly, what she was saying behind my back? And why me? I thought that as my mentor, she wanted to see me succeed. I began to question NV's motivation. I knew that I needed to confront her about what she said and how she made me feel.

I let my emotions settle from that experience before I had a conversation with NV about my concerns. I didn't want to get emotional when I spoke to her. I needed to be calm and clear in my thoughts. When I found the right moment to approach NV, I carefully explained how she made me feel. I was conscious not to attack her. I took a mature and heartfelt approach. NV looked at me intently. She didn't interrupt me while I spoke. But her face did turn a shade of red. I couldn't get a read on what she was thinking. Was she red from embarrassment? Or was NV red with anger? I was hoping she felt bad about embarrassing me. I would have been satisfied with a simple apology. But I didn't get one. When my mentor finally spoke, she said that I needed thicker skin and shouldn't take her words so personally. And then I recall that she said something like, "Welcome to television" with a smile on her face that read as though she couldn't care less how I felt. All while implying that my chosen profession was a free pass to discredit and embarrass me.

I was in disbelief. Her response completely negated my feelings. I wanted to loudly repeat myself and tell her how stupid she had made me feel! I wanted to yell at her for humiliating me in front of my peers and people who looked up to me! But there was also a part of me that wanted to cry because I was so hurt that someone I looked up to and trusted didn't seem to care about me anymore. But I kept those emotions to myself. I looked NV in the eyes, nodded, and said okay. And then I gathered my things and walked away. My tears came when I reached the privacy of my own home and no one was around to see how hurt and defeated I felt by the woman I called my mentor.

A woman who once told me that she would champion me and advance my career now made me feel humiliated, embarrassed, belittled, and deflated. But for some strange reason, I still wanted NV's approval. I suppose it was because I once idolized this woman. There was a time when I thought she was an amazing and talented person. And she still showed moments of thoughtfulness. NV bought me gifts on my birthday and during the holidays. When I got a flat tire, I called her, and she came to pick me up off the side of the road. And when I was sick with a fever, she brought me "sick food" while I recovered. But for every nice thing that NV did, she confused my psyche by doing something that was hurtful. Eventually her kindnesses were overshadowed by her cruelty. Some days she would call me on my way into work and tell me that she heard whispers in the industry that I might lose my job. She offered this piece of information on and off for almost three years. And while I suppose a forewarning of your possible demise allows you to be prepared, NV always seemed to have poor timing. Her reports often came right before one of my interviews or an important presentation. She seemed to plant a seed of worry when I needed to be focused on something more important. And when a gossip blog wrote something nasty about me (which I never took the time to read on my own), NV would forward the mean comments to me. It was so counterintuitive of what I thought a mentor should do. I spent many nights in angst over NV's hurtful behavior. But then I became forgiving every time she offered up a nice gesture.

I began to notice a theme with NV's wicked ways. Her hurtful words always presented themselves in direct correlation with my career. My birthdays were recognized with kindness. My career was criticized with meanness. And then one day I gave her a chance to redeem herself. All while hoping that I might win the approval that I longed for. I was on my way home from an out of town trip. Upon landing, I was scheduled to interview two actors for a workshop in front of a live audience. I always prepared my own interviews, and so I put the finishing touches on my presentation during the flight home. When I arrived at the auditorium for the interview, I ran into NV. I wasn't surprised to see her at the workshop because she had told me that she would come to support me. NV was aware that this was an important interview for me. I was hoping to use this interview as a sample interview for a national program on which I wanted exposure.

To my surprise, NV had prepared some information and research for my presentation. I hadn't asked her to do this research. So when I was handed the information that NV had collected, I felt honored that this successful woman took the time to help me when nothing was in it for her. I thought I was fully prepared for the interview and didn't really need NV's input. But with my mentor's gesture, my need for her approval resurfaced. I looked over the information NV had gathered and studied it. Everything looked great! Everything except one piece of information about one of the actors. Something about it didn't read right to me. I questioned NV about that information. She insisted that her research was correct and that I should use the information in my interview. My mentor was a veteran. And she was still more established than me. I chose to trust her.

The curtain went up. I introduced the two actors to the live audience. And the interview began. It was fun. It was interactive. Everyone was engaged and in good spirits. And then it came time to talk about the one piece of information that I had questioned with NV. I hesitated in my mind for a moment before I spoke. Even though my mentor had been cutting me down in front of others, I still wanted her praise. NV had insisted that all of her information was correct. I didn't want to dismiss the work she prepared and went out of her way to give to me. So I went for it. I put the information out there in front of the live audience. I knew immediately that I had made a mistake. The mood in the room changed. The actor's body language changed. It was an awkward moment in front of a live crowd. It was my belief that NV just sabotaged me to fail. Every fiber of my being was on fire! I was burning up inside and struggled to get past the concept of what had just happened.

The actors continued talking, but my thoughts were roadblocked. I wasn't sure how I was going to continue because the thoughts in my mind were like a skipping record: "I should have known not to trust her! She did this on purpose to make me fail in front of others! Why didn't I trust my instincts? I should have gone with my own research. That miserable woman knew this was an important moment for me, and she just sabotaged me!"

I did my best to recover and move on. After the workshop, one of the actors pulled me off to the side. He made it clear that I had embarrassed him with bad information. I felt awful. And it was certainly not my intention to embarrass anyone. That was not how I operated. I apologized profusely. He accepted my apology. But the damage that my mentor caused was complete. NV just threw me off the cliff and stood at the top of the mountain to watch me fall.

As the auditorium cleared, I was one of the last people in the room. While I was gathering my things, I sensed the approach of someone behind me. I turned around. It was her. My now former mentor. I stared at NV and said nothing. I have no idea what my face looked like. But I think it's fair to say that I was thinking, "You bitch!" I could barely stand to look at her. I lost my respect for this woman I once looked up to. I continued to stare right into her eyes. And then this woman who symbolized the devil on my back spoke. As I recall the encounter, her patronizing tone told me that I should have done more thorough research and then I wouldn't have looked like a fool. She continued to speak without giving me an apology. I don't believe that this woman wanted to apologize. Instead, I felt that she wanted to gloat during my fallen moment.

As I remember it, NV reminded me that I would never be as talented as she was. She told me that I couldn't outshine her, and that if I tried, I would fail. This woman definitely had power. The power to humiliate and sabotage me in front of others. I learned two facts on that day. The first fact: trust yourself, trust your instincts. The second fact: NV was filled with envy. It became apparent to me that this woman did not like to see me succeed and that she took pleasure in my failures. As the days and months unfolded after that encounter, I realized that I had learned many lessons that I needed to pass on to other women about the importance of women mentoring women.

Several days after that incident, I was babysitting my young nieces. I looked at them in wonder at their imaginative and creative minds. They were showing me pictures of their first day of school. In the pictures, my nieces held up poster boards saying what they wanted to be when they grew up. One wanted to be a photographer. The other wanted to be a painter. Standing before me were two small and impressionable little girls. While they were detailing the reasons why they wanted to be a photographer and a painter, I made sure to tell them that they were smart and creative. I told them that they could be anything that they wanted to be when they grew up. I knew that one day both little girls would become young women. As young women, they would look up to someone to help shape their careers.

I hope that their mentors will be people of positive influence. After our "what do you want to be when you grow up" talk, we popped in a Disney movie. My nieces chose the original *Snow White and the Seven Dwarfs*. Of course we all know the story of the wicked queen who asks the magic mirror on the wall, "Who is the fairest of them all?" And when the wicked queen discovers that she is not the fairest in the land but that Snow White is the fairest, the older queen does everything in her power to get rid of Snow White. Apparently this plot transcends time.

Was there a competition between me and my mentor that I was not aware of? Did my mentor want to be considered the most talented, the most wanted, and the best at her job? Did my mentor perceive me as someone who might outshine her? When I received more recognition in my profession than my mentor, did it make her jealous? Was there an invisible mirror that my mentor was looking into, wishing to be the most loved in the land of power and influence? Was I trying to dance with the devil on my back? I was. And I couldn't succeed in that story line unless I got the devil off my back and found a new mentor. My wicked mentor was abusing her power. NV lost sight of the positive influence that she could instill through the role she was given. A woman who had the ability to nurture confidence, strength, and wisdom through positive mentoring failed at her job. Instead, she created painful experiences. As I matured and became a successful woman in my professional life, I learned something very valuable. Women mentoring women is one of the most important roles in the workplace. I think that former Secretary of State Madeline Albright said it best when she spoke at a luncheon in front of the WNBA's All-Decade Team in 2006. Secretary Albright said, "There is a special place in hell for women who don't help other women." What a powerful statement. Why is it important for women to help other women? When women support women, they empower each other. When women hire other women in the workplace, they give those women an opportunity to advance their careers. When women use their wisdom and power of influence to further the career of another woman, they open a door for that woman to achieve great success. So why is it that women often want to tear down other women? We criticize the way other women look, the way they dress, the way they talk, the way they carry themselves, and even their level of success. It's not often that I hear a man with an envious tone say, "How did he get that job?" Yet I've often heard women question whether or not another woman is qualified for her position. I rarely hear men criticize other men for their choice in clothing. But I'll hear women say, "Did you see what she was wearing today?" with the implication that it was not at all fashionable.

Women are hardest on women. Why is this? Is it because they are insecure? Is it because they feel a need to compare themselves with other women? Is it because women feel that they are in competition with each other? Is it because of envy and jealousy? Maybe it's all of the above. What I do know is that when women are confident in themselves, they do not tear down other women or try to work against them. When women are secure with who they are, they want to help other women find the same sense of confidence. So when women mentor other women, it can be an amazing formula for success.

Initially my experience with a woman who failed in her role as a mentor left me convinced that I would never seek out a female mentor again. I assumed that all women liked to see other women fail in business. But that was an unfair assumption. That was just one example in my life of a woman who abused her power of influence. Not all women are this way. I thought of other female mentors in my life who used their influence in positive ways. The first female mentor from my past who comes to mind is a woman named Kathy. Kathy was the wife of a former NFL player who decided that after her husband's retirement, she wanted to get into television. I interned on a talk show one summer and was paired up with Kathy. She was a producer. I was her intern. Kathy was a Texas girl with a thick accent, and over time, "y'all" became a common word used by everyone in our office. That summer, Kathy took me under her wing and opened professional doors for me. She introduced me to people of influence. She gave me professional responsibilities and trusted that I would do a good job. And Kathy asked me about my professional goals and coached me on how to achieve them. During my internship, Kathy was building my confidence. This female mentor treated me as if I was going to do great things one day. It was a priceless gift to a twenty-year-old young woman. And it became the gift that kept on giving. I knew after Kathy's mentoring experience that I wanted to mentor others the same way. When I was finally in a position to hire interns, I made a conscious effort to train, support, and believe in the young women and men who worked for me. Watching these young people go on to do great things was very rewarding for me. I saw my former interns go on to be broadcast journalists, work for network television, and command top-level public relations positions. I even hired some of my interns after graduation. I was so proud of each and every young person I mentored. And when they told me that I had a positive influence on the direction of their careers, it was the greatest compliment I could receive.

When I thought about another positive female mentor in my life, a television journalist named Sarah popped into my mind. I met Sarah during my years as a traveling entertainment reporter. Sarah was a star in her hometown and a veteran journalist. She traveled the world and conducted high-caliber interviews with Hollywood's elite. Eventually Sarah started working behind the scenes and became a mentor to future journalists. One day Sarah called me out of the blue. She was aware of my work and always complimented me on my talents. A film organization that we were both affiliated with was about to shoot an entertainment pilot show out west. The producers of that show were looking for a host. Sarah called me because she thought I would be perfect for the job. This successful on-air journalist was now in a position to lift up another woman in the business. I flew to the studios out west and shot the pilot episode. Sarah was with me in the studio. She coached and praised me the entire time. This talented woman made me feel like I was the most talented person in the room. I'll never forget her kindness and what she did for my confidence. It was a lesson I made sure to pass on to other aspiring broadcasters.

When we're lucky, we come across a teacher we never forget. I found this teacher while I attended an all-girls high school. Her name was Donna Sheridan. I first had Mrs. Sheridan as my British literature teacher. I was never an A student. But I loved my English classes! Yet I never felt like the most outstanding student in the class. One day while I was hanging out in the hallways at school, Mrs. Sheridan approached me and told me that

I should sign up for her advanced writing class. I smiled and said that I would look into it. But inside I was so surprised that a teacher went out of her way to ask me to be in her class. And it was a class with the word "advanced" in the title! I couldn't believe that someone thought I had the brains and the talent for that kind of class. I signed up for Mrs. Sheridan's advanced writing class. And I loved every minute of that course! This teacher, who I will never forget, made me feel smart, special, and gifted. The moment Mrs. Sheridan asked me to be a part of her advanced writing class was the moment that I believed I was a good writer. It just proves how much power lies behind positive and encouraging words. On my graduation day, Mrs. Sheridan gave me a book of poetry. Inside the book she wrote, "She weaves with words a gown of wonders." Beautiful words with endless possibilities. And that is exactly what a mentor should instill in the person he or she is teaching...that there are endless possibilities.

My bad mentor and good mentors taught me great lessons about mentoring. A mentor will feed your mind with positive thoughts. Anyone who feeds you with negative thoughts about yourself is not a mentor. A good mentor will help you grow personally and professionally. Anyone who prohibits your growth is not a mentor. A great mentor will bring opportunities your way. Anyone who does not offer you opportunities or encourages you to chase opportunities is not a mentor. Align yourself with people who support you and believe in you. Do not seek the influence of people who are willing to see you collapse and fail. Look for the hand that pulls you up. Not the one that holds you down. And when the devil is on your back, shake it out.

four

He Loves Me, He Loves Me Not

Playlist Song & Artist: "I Don't Believe You" P!nk

"Prince Charming"..."Mr. Perfect"..."The One"...these words are used as terms of endearment when it comes to describing the man of our dreams. We all have our own specific descriptions of what "happily ever after" looks like. Whether he's a tall, dark, and handsome pilot who sends you jet-setting all over the world during the week and orders in fine dining takeout on the weekends. Or the all-American athletic type who provides a comfortable home in the suburbs and plays catch with your kids in the front yard. The desire for "happily ever after" exists in most of us.

I grew up with my vision of a perfect relationship. My parents seemed to be happy and in love after decades of marriage. I'm sure they had their arguments, issues, and challenges. I know that most couples do. But as their daughter, I never saw that side of their relationship. My parents were always loving and respectful of each other in front of me and my siblings. My mom and dad grew up in the same hometown and went to the same high school. My dad was popular in school and the president of his senior class. He was a handsome Italian guy who played football, basketball, and baseball. When my dad was a senior, my mom was a freshman. My mom was a beautiful brunette with deep blue eyes and a slender build. She was smart and always focused on her studies. My mom was a member of the school choir and yearbook staff. And she proudly told me that she was also a hall monitor. I laughed when I found out that she was a hall monitor. This explains why she speaks in a quiet tone and is always a rule follower.

My mom and dad didn't know each other well in high school. They were set up on a date through mutual friends years later when my dad was in dental school and my mom was in nursing school. They fell in love, got married, and over a span of eight years had three children. When my mom tells the story, she says my dad almost missed out on the opportunity to have the bride of his dreams. The evening my dad was planning to propose, he was late picking up my mom for their date. My mom was never the type to wait around for anyone, so she left her house and went about her own business that evening. When she returned home, my dad was waiting for her. With a ring. Thank goodness she said yes.

I remember as a young girl that my parents often went out on the weekends for date night and dinner with friends. Every year they would take a vacation together, just as a couple. They golfed together, attended theater performances regularly, and to this day remain season ticket holders for Cleveland Orchestra concerts. They did most, if not all, of their activities as a couple. And my parents would say that they were best friends. When I talk to my parents about how they knew that they wanted to marry each other, their answer was simple. They said that they both came from similar family backgrounds, they enjoyed each other's company, and they loved each other. They never talked about the kind of house they wanted to live in or the lavish trips they wanted to take. They didn't discuss the number of children they wanted or how much money they made. They just enjoyed each other's company and had a lot in common. It was that simple.

And it was obvious to everyone around them that they were in love. My dad would often look at my mom as if she was the most beautiful woman in the world, whether she was in her thirties or sixties. In my father's eyes, my mother's beauty was timeless. And every time my dad talked about being married to the most beautiful woman in the world, my mom would giggle like a schoolgirl and beam from ear to ear. They were happy. They were comfortable. They were best friends. And after many years of marriage, they still loved each other.

My parents set the bar high for the type of relationship I hoped for. But there is nothing wrong with that, is there? Shouldn't we want a healthy, happy, and loving relationship? And why would we settle for anything less? I found that relationships are a learning process. For me, relationships became a repetition of trial and error. Relationships of the heart begin simple and pure and become more complicated the older we get. It all starts with a crush. My first real crush happened when I was in fifth grade. His name was Lane. He was in fourth grade. We were standing in the hallway, lined up with our classmates, waiting to enter the school auditorium for an assembly. Lane was a few inches shorter than me with dark brown hair, hazel eyes, and long, thick eyelashes. He was wearing a blue button-down shirt and black polyester pants. I looked right at Lane and thought he was the cutest boy in school. I was a year older, so I took it upon my eleven-year-old self to inquire about this fourth-grade boy and his interest in me. Eventually we spent time talking about whatever grade school kids talk about together. And we would meet up at places like the local mall or roller-skating rink. I remember the first time Lane asked me to skate with him. We held hands and probably skated to a sappy eighties love song like "Say You, Say Me" by Lionel Richie or

"Take My Breath Away" by Berlin while the mirrored ball in the middle of the roller rink beamed flashing lights across the wooden floor. Lane became my first boyfriend. And the first boy to give me a love letter. Lane was my boyfriend on and off from fifth to eighth grade. And he is the first boy with whom I french kissed. Of course I needed verbal instruction from a friend on how to perform this kind of kiss because the idea of kissing with my tongue confused me and kind of grossed me out. Lane and I ended up going to different high schools and developed crushes on other people. But I'll never forget my first pure and innocent crush. It was what they called "puppy love." We all have one of those. And we never forget them.

Next came my high school boyfriend. His name was Scott, but his friends at school called him Scooter. He was tall and skinny with brown hair and tanned skin. I never thought I was one of the cute or popular girls, so when I found out that a high school boy had his eyes set on me, I was so excited! Scott was a year older than me in school and had his driver's license. He used to pick me up on Fridays in his baby-blue Oldsmobile Cutlass Ciera and take me to a place called Midway Oh Boy, home of the "Famous Oh Boy Sandwiches." There were individual jukeboxes in each restaurant booth. Scott would give me a few quarters to pick out some music. We ate our saucy burger sandwiches and fries while talking about the latest high school gossip. And when we finished our meals, we headed to the local high school football game. We would sit on the bleachers together, and when I got cold, he put his letter jacket over my shoulders and wrapped his arm around me. I felt so special.

Scott played baseball, and I made sure to attend all of his baseball games. High school relationships are a time when you celebrate every milestone. And in high school, a milestone includes your six-month anniversary of dating. For our six-month anniversary, Scott dropped off a Mylar balloon and stuffed animal on my back porch so that I would see the gift first thing in the morning before school. Again, I felt so loved and special. Eventually we broke up, and that relationship became an old memory of homecoming and prom pictures boxed away in my parents' attic.

My college dating years started off strong. I met a swimmer named Jay. He had blond hair and was Adonis-like. Jay was a top-level athlete with a beautiful figure, attractive features, and one of the nicest guys I knew in college. He always treated me with respect. But our college romance only lasted a couple of semesters and ended quietly. Eventually I became distracted by the fraternity boys around me. And from there began my poor decision making with men. After Jay, I never had a boyfriend in title throughout college. But I spent plenty of time pining over fraternity boys who only seemed interested in me for a time. Somewhere between the bongs they were hitting and the other sorority girls they were tapping, I lost my sense of self-worth. I didn't sleep around, that wasn't my style. But I did cry over guys who didn't give me the time of day or treat me with respect. I did hang around and linger to get a guy's attention even after he moved on to someone else. And I did relentlessly inquire about a boy I liked, hoping for clues that he still had feelings for me. And then when some of these same guys decided that they were interested in me again, I let them walk back into my life only to disrespect me all over again.

I remember sitting with one of my girlfriends on the back patio of our house. We were both moping over boys who were acting like dirtbags. We pulled flowers from one of the potted plants on the patio and starting plucking the petals...he loves me...he loves me not. We repeated the phrase until the last petal was plucked. Of course we were playing this flower game in jest. But we didn't need a flower to tell us how these college boys felt about us. Isn't it obvious when a boy makes you cry and question your own self-worth?

We all have pivotal relationships in our lives. Some that affect us in positive ways. And some that hurt us in terrible ways. We want to be in good, healthy relationships. But I talk to so many women who find themselves stuck in unhealthy relationships. And they're stuck by choice. Why do we choose to stay in a bad relationship? Why do we cry over a man who doesn't want us? Why do we hold out hope that one day he'll change his mind? Why don't we want to believe him when he says that he doesn't want us anymore? And why do we wait until we're out of a bad relationship to ask ourselves these questions? I'm guilty of all of this. And I had a great example of a loving relationship growing up. My dad was a nice guy, and my mom didn't want to wait around for him when he was only fifteen minutes late! And it was already established that he was in love with her. I discovered that I didn't inherit that sense of confidence from my mother. When it came to bad relationships, I waited around.

I first met Ken when I was in my midtwenties and working to build my career. Ken was around my age and in sales. I call him Ken because he actually looked like a Ken doll. He was tall and had a slender but athletic build. His teeth were perfectly straight, although he should have used Crest white strips to lighten his coffee-tinted teeth! Ken's cheekbones were chiseled, and each side of his face appeared to be symmetrical to the other. His hair was light brown and always trimmed short. Ken's eyes were a hazel hue, but he was color blind and so his clothes and socks were often mismatched. And after a year of knowing each other, we became a mismatched couple. Ken was gorgeous, but he wasn't the brightest guy. He was prettier than me, but I could talk circles around him as I was well read and he never picked up a book. I was raised to be classy and respectful toward others. Ken was from a likable family who admittedly didn't have finesse. As a result, Ken often said awkward things in public.

I'll never forget the time we stopped by my parents' house for a quick visit. My mom and dad were on their way to a charity ball. My dad was dressed in a tuxedo, my mom in a beautiful gown. As I remember it, the moment Ken saw my parents he said, "Hey, Pops, are you taking her to a strip club?" I was mortified. My parents just laughed uncomfortably for a second. I knew that Ken often made inappropriate comments, but when he said things like that in front of my parents, I was embarrassed. I suppose I was just attracted to Ken's looks. Intellectually he didn't do anything for me. There was a disconnect when we would talk, and he didn't have a lot of depth. But I still chose to spend three years dating Ken. And during those three years, I lost a part of myself to a guy who was not good for me.

When you find yourself in a long-term relationship, you feel invested in that relationship. Even if you're not happy and you have little in common, you've devoted your time and energy to that person. You become comfortable. You become complacent. You hate the idea of going through the get-to-know-you phase again, so you decide to take the easy route and stay put in your boring, unhappy, and unhealthy relationship. But sometimes that unhealthy relationship has a breakthrough. Sometimes that person you are committed to opens up about something personal. He shows you his weaknesses and vulnerabilities. You see this as a bonding moment. In your mind, you decide that this moment makes you more connected to each other. And every time this person treats you with disrespect, you rationalize staying in the relationship because of those few moments that you "bonded." I know this to be true because I did this with Ken.

Ken didn't handle his alcohol well. He told me that his father was an alcoholic. I can't say that Ken was too, but he was a mean drunk. I was usually Ken's designated driver because I didn't party to the extent that he did. And the one time that I trusted him to drive was a night that I thought I might die. The roads were unfamiliar to me and they were winding. Ken had no business being behind the wheel of a car. But I had no idea where I was, and he threatened to leave me stranded. So I got in his car. It was the most terrifying ride of my life. It was fast. It was dark. And I thought the car might tip over a few times. To this day, it takes my breath away every time I think back to that car ride. I should have let him leave me. I should have called the police. I should have fought him for the keys. But I got in the car. I survived. We both did. But I never put myself in that situation again.

For the first year that we dated, I didn't know much about Ken's childhood. I tried to get him to open up about his younger years, but it was difficult to peel back the layers of his past. In time, I learned little bits about his early years. He told me that his father used to hit his mother and his brothers when he would come home drunk. Ken was the youngest in his family. As a little boy, he told me that he would hide in the basement closet when his dad came home so that he could avoid being the victim of his father's fist. He curled up into a ball and cried when he told me that story. He reminded me of a scared child who was hiding from the monster in the dark. It was one of the few times he ever got emotional in front of me. He hugged me tightly and told me that he loved me. He told me that I was the best thing that ever happened to him. I was shocked to hear those words because there seemed to be a disconnect between us. But I also felt special when he told me that he loved me and confided in me. I felt we'd had a breakthrough. And I translated Ken's breakdown into meaning that we were more connected in our relationship.

One afternoon I decided to have a friend over to my apartment for a cookout. Ken was staying at my place that weekend, and I wanted him to meet my friend. I prepared some food ahead of time so that I had more time to visit with my company. After my kitchen prep, I joined Ken on the couch to relax before my friend came over. I tried to engage in conversation with Ken, but he didn't seem interested in talking to me. In fact, I recall him ignoring me altogether while he sipped on his beer. His silence irritated me, and I persisted in trying to talk to him. After a couple years of dating this guy, I longed for more engaging conversations. I'm not sure how the next chain of events started, but it felt like an out-of-body experience for me. Ken went from silence to rage. One moment we were sitting next to each other on the couch in silence, and the next thing I knew, we were doing a violent dance from room to room. This is my recollection of how the next several minutes unfolded. His hands were clenched around my arms and his fingers were digging into me. At one point, he pressed his fist into my throat. He was pushing me up against the wall, then onto the bed and back up against the wall with force. I was screaming and crying. He was violent.

I remember thinking to myself as this moment was unfolding, "What if the neighbors hear? My mom and dad never did this. I wasn't raised to end up in an abusive relationship. I'm screaming and crying and he's hurting me. I feel like a piece of trash. I'm so embarrassed that this is happening to me. I hate him. But I don't want him to leave me. How is this happening to me?"

And then there was silence. I was pinned up against the front door. We both looked down at the white shirt I was wearing. It had blood on it. I remember Ken said to me, "That's your fault. You did that." With tears in my eyes, blood on my shirt, and scrapes on my arms, I reminded him that my friend was arriving soon for the cookout. Ken told me to change my shirt and clean up. I did what he told me to do. Moments later, my friend arrived. And together Ken and I smiled, laughed, entertained my friend, and acted as if nothing just happened. I stayed in that relationship for another year. And I never told my family what happened that day. It was a secret I planned to keep. Until now.

Eventually Ken left me. He met another girl who he said was a better match for him. I felt crushed when this first happened.

And I begged him to keep our relationship going. I didn't want to believe that he didn't want me anymore. I reminded him that no one knew him as well as I did, which of course was a bunch of emotional crap, because he was a shitty person. I cried over our breakup. I lost my appetite and didn't take care of myself. And I did the dreaded drive-by to his house.

One day when I found myself driving in the direction of Ken's address, I knew that I wanted to stop myself. So I called a friend to talk me out of going to his house. My friend didn't answer. So I called my sister. My sister didn't answer. So I tried to call my mother, but instead my father answered. He could hear the sniffles in my voice. I told him where I was heading. My dad didn't know the worst about Ken, but he was still my father, and he knew that this guy was no good for me. With clear certainty in his voice, my dad said, "Andrea, turn your car around. Ken is not right for you. Come over to our house. I'll open up a nice bottle of wine, and we can talk about this. But you are to never call that boy again. Never."

My father's words were not a suggestion. They were a command. I listened. And from that day forward, I never called or did a drive-by again.

I was hurt that Ken replaced me with someone else. But the truth is my replacement did me a huge favor. If another girl hadn't come along, I might have stayed in that abusive and unhealthy relationship longer. While my replacement seemed to be a blessing in disguise, I needed to do some soul-searching. I needed to figure out why I would stay with a man who harmed me physically and emotionally. And I needed to promise myself that I would never date a man like that again.

I spent much of the next year talking about how Ken was wrong for me. But I never got to the root of why I stayed. In order to heal, you must understand what is at the core of your pain. It was impossible for me to heal because I never took the time to understand *why* I allowed that unhealthy relationship to continue for so long. And so I left myself open and vulnerable to the next predator to come along. I was like a self-destructive Velcro wall, attracting anything bad that would stick.

I didn't date anyone seriously for a long time after Ken. I went out on dates here and there. And there were some really nice guys who came into my life. But I never felt that "spark." The spark that I saw exist between my parents and other happy couples. And then many years later, after I thought old wounds had healed, I met man I will call Hunter. And this time, I thought I found the perfect guy.

I was in my midthirties when I met Hunter. We were set up on a blind date. I was hesitant about the blind date process, but I was still single and decided to take a leap of faith. Hunter was several years old than me and had never been married. I was well established in my television career, and he was a successful businessman. Our first meeting was set up at a trendy gastropub in town. I freshened up at work after a long day of interviews and changed into a flirty skirt and conservative cotton top. I threw on my heels, not knowing how tall Hunter would be. But I figured if he was too short, it might only seem awkward if I bent down to hug him at the end of the night.

I arrived at our blind date first. So I sat at the bar and ordered a glass of red wine. About five minutes after I sat down, Hunter arrived. He was tall with dark hair that was laced with pieces of gray. His nose was pronounced and his lips were thin. His eyes were dark in color, but they seemed to be friendly. And his tanned skin showed signs of age from either sun exposure or adolescent acne. He reached out his hand to introduce himself. His hands were large and his grip was strong. Hunter was casually dressed. But I could tell his taste in clothing was impeccable. The first few minutes of a blind date are typically filled with anxious conversation. But this man had an ease about him. He was confident, animated, engaging, and fun to talk to. I made a living off of talking to people, so together we didn't miss a beat. He ordered a drink and we settled into our conversation. As the night went on, I became more attracted to Hunter as it appeared we had much in common. I enjoyed his company that evening and hoped that he would ask me out again. He did. We went on a few more dates and decided quickly that we wanted to be exclusive. Every morning on my way to work, Hunter would either call or text message me. He always wished me a good day and told me how happy he was that I was in his life. After three weeks of going on dates, I now had a new boyfriend. And everyone in my life seemed to love him.

My family members have always been the most important people in my life. I was excited to introduce them to this new man that I met. My parents, my brother, my sister, my grandparents, they all met Hunter. They all seemed to be charmed by him. Their stamp of approval was important to me. My family met some of the bad guys I dated over the years. They knew the kind of guy who was right for me. And the type of guy who was wrong for me. Hunter completely won them over! Yes, he was successful. Yes, he was mature. Yes, I was attracted to him. But he was also treating me like a prize to be won in front of my family. And privately he treated me well too. He was a gentleman. He was interested in my life and always asked me about my dreams and goals. He was loving and tender. And he often expressed that he was a family man. The new man in my life repeatedly talked about how much he loved his family. Hunter told me that every Sunday, he went to his parents' house for homemade pizza night. And he told me about all of his family traditions. Hunter often expressed his desire to have a family of his own someday. The more Hunter talked, the more I liked what he was saying.

My relationship with Hunter moved at lightning speed. After three dates we decided to become a couple. And within the first two months of dating, he met my parents, I met his parents, and our parents met each other. It was Hunter's idea to organize a dinner night for his family and my family to meet. Around this time, we started talking about our future together. We talked about marriage and children. While it seemed soon to talk about these intimate topics, I just assumed that it was normal because we were both older. And now that I was in my thirties, I had a strong desire to get married and have children. Maybe I was subconsciously rushing things, but I was just following Hunter's lead. He was the one who brought up marriage and kids. And he seemed to talk about both with no fear or hesitancy. I know that it's typically the woman who brings up marriage and children first. So when the man in my life discussed his desire for these things with me, I was quietly thrilled!

I grew into being a very independent woman. As an adult, I always had my own job. Made my own money. And bought my own things. I lugged all of my own groceries from my car to my kitchen. I took care of problems around the house. And when I was sick, I nursed myself back to health. I know how to take care of myself. But even when you're independent, it's nice to have someone take care of you every now and then. And when Hunter came along, he wanted to take care of me. I liked it. He bought me gifts. He paid for my spinning classes. He carried my groceries. And he gave me foot rubs while we watched television. It felt nice to have a man take care of me. I hadn't felt this way in a long time. And now that I had a relationship in my life, I realized how much I missed it. I made sure to tell Hunter how much I appreciated all of what he was doing for me.

Two months into our relationship, Hunter started talking to me about our wedding. We weren't engaged. And he had not proposed. But it sounded as if he was proposing a proposal. He talked about the priest who he hoped would perform the ceremony. He showed me the church where he wanted us to get married. He told me that he had a jeweler who would make my ring. And then he pulled up his iPad to have me look at ring settings. Hunter showed me what he liked and didn't like. I know it's been said that every girl dreams about her wedding day. And that she has every detail planned out in her mind. I was not that girl. I knew that I wanted to be married someday. But I never envisioned the dress, the ring, the flowers, the cake, or the invitations. I probably thought about who I wanted in my wedding. And even that changed a few times over the years. So when Hunter started talking about everything that he wanted, I was unfazed that it was all about him. I was just excited that I wasn't going to end up an old maid!

The wedding talks continued, and I started getting excited about planning the details. Hunter even asked his friend to be his best man. But this is where it gets to be strange. Hunter picked a best man, but I didn't have a proposal or a ring on my finger. Don't you need a bride-to-be before you need a best man? I chose to ignore that question in my mind and continue living out my proposed happy future. I began to fully invest my time and energy into the idea of "forever" with this man. We talked about traveling together, having children together, cooking dinner together, sleeping next to each other, and growing old together. It was decided. He was my future.

Before our future was discussed, I remember the first time we said "I love you." I said it first. We were on a flight home from a beach vacation we took after a month of dating. It was the first time in years that I took a trip with a boyfriend. After years of traveling alone, it felt so good to have a man sitting next to me holding my hand on the airplane. I was listening to some sappy music on my iPod. And looking over at Hunter, I felt overwhelmed with happiness. I leaned into him and whispered in his ear, "I love you." He smiled, kissed me, and said, "I love you too." Saying those words made me feel vulnerable. But having him say those words back to me made me feel secure, wanted, and loved.

We all have private parts of our lives that we are careful not to share with others. We all have secrets that we keep. Hunter was very communicative about his past relationships and why they didn't work out. He shared what seemed to be personal stories regarding his own demons, like a substance addiction that he battled. He talked about his life as if it was an open book. I, on the other hand, tend to me more guarded about my private matters. When we were out to dinner one night, Hunter sat across from me and acknowledged that I often seem guarded and that I needed to show him my vulnerabilities and weaknesses. He told me that if we were going to spend our lives together, I needed to trust him and open up to him. What he was saying made sense. I just didn't feel ready to share every private detail of my past. Not that my past was that juicy, but it was still my life and my story to share when I wanted and with whom I wanted. Hunter told me that he was my future and that he was the man I would be leaning on for the rest of my life. I thought about my parents and how close they were as a couple. I knew that they shared everything with each other. I wanted to be like them. And since Hunter was telling me that we were always going to be together, I decided to let my wall down, little by little.

I told Hunter about Ken. About the fight we had. And about how embarrassed I was that I stayed in an abusive relationship. I told him that I had a fear of being left. I wasn't sure where that fear came from, but I often feared that a man would change his mind and back out of making a commitment to me. I told him about my struggles with my mentor and the pain that she caused. I told him that I worried about the future of my career. There was turmoil in the television industry, and changes were taking place all around me. People were losing their jobs, and I knew that I was in a vulnerable position. I told Hunter that I worried about what would happen to my career if I ever lost my job. I told him that I wondered if I would be able to have children someday. I was getting older, and I knew there was a risk of not being able to conceive. And the entire time I talked, Hunter kept reminding me that it was okay to be vulnerable in front of him. He really wanted me to know that I could trust him and that he loved me. This experience made me feel closer to him. I was beginning to share pieces of my soul with this man. And when a woman shares her soul with a man, that man becomes a part of her soul.

As fast as my relationship with Hunter started was about the same speed with which it crumbled. I was blindsided. I barely saw it coming. But after three and a half months of dating and planning our future together, Hunter became a different person from the one I first met. Hunter got me good. And it turned out he loved me not.

The changes were subtle at first. He was clearly a dominant with his directives on how he wanted our "wedding" to play out. But at the time, I overlooked his dominance because I was so excited about the thought of getting married. He would take me out for pedicures but insisted on picking out the color for my toes. I found it strange, but I reasoned it out by deciding that it was okay for him to pick my nail polish color because he was paying for the spa service.

I gained a few pounds from all of the fabulous food that I ate at ten o'clock in the morning during cooking segments on my talk show. I wanted to lose about five to ten pounds. But when Hunter looked at pictures that showed a thinner version of me, he told me that the pictures didn't look like me and that I should never try to be that weight again. I reasoned out his request by telling myself that he loved me just the way I was, even if I had ten pounds of weight to lose. I decided Hunter was being sweet. But if I had looked at these small signs clearly, I would have seen that this dominant man wanted to control many aspects of my life. These were subtle ways for him to introduce his dominance. I chose to overlook this character flaw. And I, the independent woman, allowed him to be the dominant figure in our relationship.

Soon after the subtle changes in his personality, the more obvious changes took place. Hunter had outpatient surgery while we were dating. I picked him up from the hospital and took care of him that day. Taking care of him mostly consisted of offering water, preparing a meal, and making sure that he was comfortable. He was lying on the couch watching *SportsCenter* while icing his wounds. He kept screaming out in loud pain during the icing process. You would have thought someone stabbed him in the groin based on the painful sounds coming from his mouth. I suggested that he wrap the ice with a kitchen towel while applying it to his body. I told him that my mom, who was a nurse, used to do it that way when we were kids.

With a look of disgust on his face, I remember him saying to me, "You're so fucking ignorant! You think because your mom was a fucking nurse you know how I should treat my hand? I fucking know what I'm doing!" I was speechless. I felt as if I had just been punched in the gut. I didn't know what to say. He was in pain, and I just wanted to help him. The only words I could muster in that moment sounded sad and insecure. With sorrow on my face and in a whispered voice, I said, "I was just trying to help." And then I walked out of the room and cried to myself. I didn't want Hunter to see my tears. I was afraid that he might make me feel worse in my weak moment.

After the ice pack incident, I could sense a disconnect between us unfolding. The early-morning phone calls and text messages stopped. It was a noticeable change, and it hurt my feelings. But my days were so busy that I let it go. We didn't spend many nights together because we lived in separate apartments. And when we did spend the night together, I was often restless. I couldn't get comfortable with him next to me. I would watch him sleep, and quite honestly, I didn't feel attracted to him. He was an ugly sleeper. I just never noticed it before. When I would cook for him, he never complimented my meals (and I knew they were good). Instead, Hunter told me how his father and mother prepared their version of the dish I just cooked. I was suffering from comparison. This also hurt my feelings. Sometime that summer while we were dating, Hunter came with me to a family wedding. We were seated with my family members, including a couple of elderly cousins. Both cousins are sharp and beautiful women. And just because they were older didn't mean that they couldn't hear the words of a disrespectful man sitting next to them. Hunter started making fun of my older cousins and making inappropriate comments about them. He was rude. He was embarrassing. And he was thoughtless. These people were my family members. His comments were disrespectful to them and to me. All of these examples were adding up to a whole lot of bad news. But I stayed in the relationship. My instincts were beginning to tell me that this man was not compatible with me. But I couldn't let go of the knowledge that I once opened up to him. I allowed myself to trust him and talked about plans for a future with him. Was I going to leave him now? I should have. But I didn't. I wanted so badly for things to get better.

It was the end of May and about four months into our relationship when Hunter and I took a trip to New York City together. It was hot in the city that weekend. But we went prepared to walk everywhere and explore a city that we both loved. I hoped this trip would help us bond and get back on track to where we were a few months earlier, happy and excited about building a future together. My family didn't know that I was having doubts about Hunter. They thought Hunter might be proposing in New York. In my gut, I knew it was still too soon for that. But I also believed that this was a trip to reconnect.

Hunter seemed to have the whole weekend mapped out. He knew where he wanted to eat and shop. And I went along with his plans. We stayed at one of the trendy hotels in New York City and got a room upgrade. But it didn't matter because

I didn't plan on spending much time in the room. Manhattan is a city to soak in. There's not much time for rest when you visit New York. We walked everywhere...Upper Manhattan, Lower Manhattan, Soho, Tribeca, Central Park. I followed Hunter everywhere he wanted to go. The only stop that was on my list was a jewelry store.

A couple months ago, Hunter had told me to show him the kind of setting I wanted for an engagement ring. I really had no clue. So I thought what better place to look than at Tiffany's in New York? I didn't need or want a Tiffany's ring. I just wanted to get some ideas. During one of our excursions, we found ourselves in front of the jewelry store known for its little blue box. I pointed it out. Hunter didn't respond. In fact, he didn't seem interested in walking through the doors of that store at all. I felt stupid for suggesting that we go into a jewelry store. I didn't want to be the girl who begs for a ring. I hadn't been that girl. But after many weeks of talking to me about the ring he wanted to buy, I thought it would be okay to bring up ring shopping. Apparently it wasn't. And so we never went into Tiffany's.

We dined at some beautiful restaurants in New York. But this man who was once full of endless topics of conversation barely spoke to me during our meals. It was as though we were two people meeting for the first time who had nothing to say to each other. I tried to initiate conversation with him, but it sounded as if I was interviewing someone who didn't want to talk. His answers were never more than one sentence long. We were not enjoying each other's company. He felt like a stranger. A stranger with whom I was sharing a bed. During the Q&A portion of dinner, I eventually brought up the topic of our future together. Hunter was now ready to speak. But I was not fully prepared for what he was about to say.

Yes, there was a disconnect between us. Yes, he was showing signs that he was not the man I once trusted. Yes, I was beginning to doubt my feelings for him. And yes, I wanted so badly to have a husband and a family of my own that I chose to ignore the voice in my head and the feeling in my gut that told me Hunter was not right for me anymore. But the words Hunter was about to speak to me were so painful that I forgot that I had been doubting him for weeks. This is how I recall the conversation. Hunter told me that he was beginning to wonder if I was a selfish and thoughtless person. He told me that I always made every situation about myself and that I never took his wants or needs into consideration. He told me that he wasn't sure if he was attracted to me anymore. And he questioned whether or not he wanted a future with me. And then he went for the jugular. It was as though he had been taking notes the one night we were out to dinner and he asked me to show him my vulnerabilities and weaknesses. He told me that he wasn't surprised that Ken wanted to hit me because I was an irritating person. Hunter reminded me that I once told him that I had a fear of men leaving me. He told me that most men would probably want to leave me because I would never be good enough for anyone. And on the topic of children, Hunter told me I should probably let that dream go because it was not likely to happen for me. I stared at him in silence with tears in my eyes the entire time he spoke. At first my tears sat still, welling up between my lashes. But with every word that came from Hunter's mouth, the pain in my heart became so unbearable that my throat closed up and tears slid down my cheeks. My emotions were exposed. My fears were coming true. I couldn't believe this was happening. And when he finally finished speaking, I took a breath and said these words over and over: "You said that you loved me. You promised me that you wanted to marry me. You told me that you would not leave me. You said that you wanted to have children with me. You told me that I could be vulnerable in front of you. You told me that I could trust you. You made promises to me. You promised me. Why did you promise me?"

I sat at that outdoor restaurant on the street of New York City in shock. I couldn't believe what Hunter was saying. I didn't want to believe him. For months I allowed myself to believe in this man and his words. I trusted him when he told me that he loved me and wanted a future with me. I let my guard down with him and shared pieces of my soul with him. And now all of the fears I had shared with him were coming true. In that moment, I felt as if it was his plan to hurt me to my core. It appeared as though the hunter had found his prey. I felt beaten. Broken. Exposed. Abandoned. Unwanted. Undesirable. Weak. Ugly. And dead inside. This man once claimed to love me. And now he loved me not.

When I first heard P!nk sing "I Don't Believe You," it was from a video clip after her appearance on *Oprah*. I added this song to my playlist because it spoke to my heartache. The lyrics were painful, and I identified with that feeling of not wanting to believe someone when he told me that he didn't love me anymore. If you've ever been heartbroken, listen to this song. It cuts to the core of your heartache. But the more I thought about the lyrics, the more I thought about the message I wanted to convey in this chapter. Instead of saying "I don't believe you," we should be saying "I must believe myself." We have to listen to that voice in our head and that feeling in our gut when we sense that something is wrong. When Ken was abusive, I knew he was a bad guy. I knew I was in an unhealthy relationship. But even before our fight, I knew that we were not compatible. We didn't have anything in common. I should have believed myself when I knew that we were mismatched. And when Hunter began to show a change in his personality, I ignored those signs because I was so focused on wanting a husband. I didn't pay attention to the fact that he became a man who didn't make me feel good. He stopped making me happy. And eventually he preyed upon my weaknesses. I wish I'd had the courage to walk away and know that he was not the right man for me.

But staying in an unhealthy relationship all comes back to the reason *why*. Why did I stay? Why does anyone stay? If you were on the outside looking into a toxic relationship that your friend, sister, mother, or daughter was involved in, you would tell her to leave. I know I have done that with many friends in my life. So when I look back at my own situation, I try to look at it through someone else's eyes. My parents' eyes. I imagine they would say to me, "We told you that you were beautiful, smart, talented, and kind. Why would you ever let a man treat you this way? We raised you in a happy and healthy home. Why wouldn't you want the same for yourself? We did everything that we could to build your confidence. Why would you let someone tear you down? You're such an independent woman. Why wouldn't you walk away?" And just maybe my father would say, "You should have kicked him in the balls and never looked back."

Every time these men treated me unkindly, I sent a message that their behavior was acceptable by not leaving them. And so their bad behavior became a manipulative and vicious cycle. I stayed because I lost confidence in myself. I stayed because I wasn't sure if anyone else would come along, and so I chose to settle. I stayed because I thought they needed me and that made me feel wanted. I needed to feel wanted. I stayed because I didn't want to be alone. I didn't really enjoy their company, but I feared that bad company was better than no company at all. I stayed for all the wrong reasons. I shared pieces of my heart and soul with these unhealthy men. And over time I forgot who I was raised to be...confident, happy, healthy, and independent. I felt none of those things when I was in unhealthy relationships.

When I looked back on my relationships, I found there were a couple of important lessons to be learned. The first thing I discovered was that I needed a man's attention to feel good about myself. Of course we all want to be noticed and desired. But relying on a man to make us feel good about ourselves is a mistake.

My need for a man's attention caused me to attract the wrong guys. When I was needy and insecure, I attracted men who fed those weaknesses. Whereas if I was confident and comfortable with myself, I believe I would have attracted men who appreciated my strengths. The saying is true, even in relationships, that you get what you pay for. When you treat yourself as if you're cheap and weak, you get junk. But when you showcase your God-given assets, you will be rewarded. Be the best of who you are. You will attract the same kind of people.

The other lesson I learned from experiencing unhealthy relationships is that it's always important to trust your instincts. In both of my bad relationships, I knew in my gut that something was wrong with the men I was dating. I chose to ignore my instincts. Your instincts will rarely let you down. When you sense that someone isn't compatible with you, he or she probably isn't. When you sense that someone seems controlling, his or her power to control you will become stronger over time. When someone makes you feel bad about yourself, he or she does not love you. Repeat that thought to yourself. If someone makes you feel bad about yourself, he or she does not love you. I know it hurts. I know you don't want to believe that it's true. But you don't want to commit your heart to someone who does not love you.

Know this to be true. Bad men can only manipulate you if you're a good person. I don't believe that a manipulator can manipulate another manipulator. The only way to beat unhealthy people at their own game is to stop playing their game. Remove yourself from the situation. Bad people are good at what they do. They know what they are doing. And if you have a good heart and soul, the only way to win the battle is to say good-bye. And never look back.

We must believe in ourselves. We must believe that we are good enough for only the best in life. We must believe that we are strong enough to walk away from anyone who treats us poorly. We must believe that when we feel broken, we will heal. And we must believe that anyone who tries to break us is not someone who loves us. It's okay to walk away. Believe that you are worth only the best and that someone good and kind will love you. And that starts with loving yourself.

five

Always Get Back Up

Playlist Song & Artist: *"The Climb" Miley Cyrus*

The Oscars reminded me of one of life's great lessons. And let's be honest, the Academy Awards can be a very boring show. At least that's my opinion. But one of my favorite moments happened during the 2013 Oscars broadcast. It wasn't my favorite moment because it was a laughable, well-scripted, or particularly poignant moment. I loved this moment for what it symbolized. I was sitting on my couch in cozy sweats with a bowl of crunchy snack food on my lap and chocolate-covered blueberries within reach. After investing hours of my time in front of the television set, it was nearing the later part of the show where the Academy Award for best actress was about to be handed out.

"And the Oscar goes to...Jennifer Lawrence for *Silver Linings Playbook*," was announced. Lawrence was a young, rising star, and this was her first Oscar win. As she walked toward the stage in her beautiful Dior designer gown, Lawrence tripped and fell on the steps leading up to the grand stage. It was her big moment in front of Hollywood and the world...and she fell! In Dior!

Lawrence took two seconds to compose herself, picked herself up off the steps, walked to the microphone, and in front of everyone watching, made a quick joke about her fall and moved on with her acceptance speech. She was embarrassed. She was surprised. She was joyful. And she was thankful. But even better than all of those things, she got back up. The message was simple. When you fall, get back up.

I never thought that would happen to me. Have you ever spoken those words? In your lifetime, you've probably observed the struggles of other people. Divorce. Job loss. Abusive relationships. Loss of a child. Addictions. Or tragedy in some form or another. But when we're on the outside of someone's life and looking in, the view can seem so far removed from what's happening in our own lives. When someone struggles, we feel sympathy. But we often thank God that it's not us. When struggles happen to someone we love, we want to take away that person's pain. But when we are the ones struggling, we want to throw our hands in the air and say, "Hey, God, what else do you have for me? What's next?" As if to imply that we've had enough uphill battles and need divine intervention to give us a break. Sometimes we are just plain tired of being tough. I had five consecutive weeks in my life when I faced my greatest challenges and struggles. Five weeks don't seem like a lot of time in an entire lifetime. But I was throwing my hands in the air, wondering how much more I would have to take. I was on my knees, wishing the struggles would end. I had fallen, and I wasn't sure how to get back up.

At the time of my five-week fall, I was a thirty-six-year-old woman who had never been married and didn't have children. I was living an independent life, but I never imagined in my early twenties that I would become a career woman without a family of my own. Life had a different plan for me. I found myself jet-setting all over the world, interviewing celebrities and spending late nights talking about films with my fellow broadcast colleagues while sipping great wines at swanky hotels. Most of my days were filled with television research and preparing for my live talk show. And my nights continued with more research and preparation for my job. I rarely had a free weekend due to either travel for work or hosting charity events. My job consumed my life. And this was all happening by choice. I chose this career. I was fully committed to this career. And even though it wore me down many times, I kept plugging away. I really couldn't see myself doing anything else. But anytime you work for someone other than yourself, there is always a chance that you might lose your job. No matter how committed or productive you are.

WEEK ONE of my big fall. It was a beautiful spring day in May. I remember driving to work that day admiring the blue skies and a few puffy clouds. I didn't sleep well the night before, but the morning sunshine gave me an extra ounce of energy to start my day. I went about my usual business that day, but was later called into an unexpected meeting in a conference room on the third floor of my building. I walked into the room and was met by my boss. She had bad news. After thirteen years of hard work and doing my best to be a productive, dedicated employee, I was told that I was losing my job, with the option to keep working for two more weeks. I wasn't losing my job because I did anything wrong. It was just the nature of my business. It was the first time I ever lost a job. And I felt as if I had lost my identity. I was now unemployed. No incoming paychecks. No health benefits. No reason to set my alarm at six o'clock in the morning. And no clue how to answer the question "What do you do for work?" when someone asked. I was out of work. And I was ashamed to say so. Not to mention I had a career that was in the public eye, so questions about my television job were endless. The day I lost my job, I called my mom from my apartment. I was sitting in a fetal position underneath the windowsill. I tried to sound tough when I delivered the news. But without warning, I launched into a hyperventilating type of crying. And I remember saying between tears and deep breaths, "I have no husband. I have no children. And now I have no job." In that moment, I thought I saw my life flash before me. I thought about my choice of focusing on my career and not on my personal life. I wondered if it was the right choice. Especially now that I had nothing to show for it. At least that's what I thought at the time. My mom allowed me to cry out my worries, and then in a supportive tone, she reminded me that it was time to embrace the next chapter in my life. It was a chapter that I had known would come eventually.

To be honest, I had sensed my job was ending. Most people who work on the air in television have an expiration date. For some, their contract ends after a few years and they move on to the next job. For others, they find success in their television market and stay on the air for decades. I never had a contract. And for months, I heard whispers about my show being cancelled. And so the day that my boss gave me my two weeks' notice, I was not shocked. Although internally I was thinking, "Oh shit, oh shit, oh shit, oh shit. This is real. What am I going to do now?"

I had the option to end my employment the day after I received the fateful news. I went with that option. I wanted to go on the air to say good-bye to the viewers and thank them for their loyalty. I still remember everything about the last day of the first job I was let go from. I was wearing a black cotton top and a bright orange skirt. I had played Kid Rock's "Bawitdaba" on repeat as I drove into work that morning. There was nothing sentimental about the song. It was loud. It was rock. And I didn't understand what some of the words meant. I think that's why the song kept my emotions steady. And that's what I needed. I needed to be steady that day. My awareness of my surroundings was astute. I remember all of the conversations I had that morning at work. I knew they were going to be my last conversations on that day, at that location, in my current position. I remember taking mental snapshots of the television studio that day because it would be my last time in the studio as the host of that morning show. The only part of the day that is somewhat of a blur to me was my on-air good-bye speech. I didn't rehearse anything, nor did I have the words written in teleprompter. I spoke from the heart. I thanked the viewers. I thanked my cohost and coworkers. And I thanked my family. It took me seven minutes to say thank you and good-bye. And if I really want to be reminded of what I said, I can still find the clip on YouTube where it will likely live forever. As I drove away from the building on the last day of my job, I was still thinking, "Oh shit, oh shit, oh shit. What am I going to do now?"

I was contacted by the local press to be interviewed about my departure. The first question asked was, "Were you fired?" It became a common question. I was still trying to wrap my brain around what happened. I wasn't ready to reveal everything about a very private and painful time in my life. My instincts were to retreat into hiding. But the best response that I could offer was to say that it was my choice to leave the day I left. That was the truth. I did choose to leave the show that day. It just wasn't the full truth. But that was all I felt comfortable revealing during a very private time in my life. And my former employer respected my delicate position by backing up my take on my departure. I knew that I had to look for another job. But I was feeling beaten. During this time, I wanted to turn to family and close friends for support.

WEEK TWO of my big fall. I was licking my wounds from losing my job and turning to friends and family for moral support. I had one specific friend who had been in my life for a long time. This friend was someone I leaned on during life's bumps in the road. We shared personal stories about our lives. We took part in each other's family celebrations. And we were always loyal to our friendship. We were close. Like family. Or so I thought. I was about to be kicked while I was down. By someone I trusted. One week after I lost my job, I was told that this close friend had been backstabbing me for months with unkind comments and stories of gossip. I didn't want to believe it when I heard the news. But while I was struggling, this friend was nowhere to be found. After my last day of work, one week passed...then two...then two months...then many more months... and still no word from this friend. I believe my greatest strength is my loyalty. Some might say my greatest weakness is expecting the same in return. I don't do well with betrayals. Then again, who does? This particular friend was someone who I helped break into the television industry. I helped this person get a job. I championed this person. I fought for this person. I was loyal to this person. And I loved this person as a friend. I shared secrets and personal information with this person. Together we cried, laughed, and shared our dreams. Somewhere along the way, unbeknownst to me, this friendship became one-sided. Meaning I was the only one in it. I was told that this person openly made negative comments about me and chose to divulge many of the private conversations we had to other people. It took me a long time to reach out to this former friend and tell this person what I learned. Of course there are always two sides to a story. My former friend denied the information I was given. I have no proof of what was said or not said. What I do know for a fact is that this person abandoned my side when I needed a good friend. This person was nowhere to be found when I lost my job. Betrayals can happen. And it's painful when they do. Especially when it happens with someone you love and care for. My knowledge of this betrayal came one week after I lost my job. The timing was not great. No job. A bad friend. My confidence was taking a beating.

WEEK THREE of my big fall. I was dumped. Yes, by the same guy in the last chapter. Tossed out like yesterday's news. Rejected by a man who promised me the world. You know who he is. The kind of guy who paints a picture of your happy life together. The one who makes you a list of promises that you swear he's going to keep. The kind of guy who often seems too good to be true. And then you find out that he's actually a piece of crap. You now think he's the worst thing that ever happened to you. He lies. He makes you cry. He makes you feel insecure. He's mean. He's become a different person from the one you first knew. After I lost my job, I was fully focused on my relationship. I put all of my energy into the idea of forever with the man I was dating. I thought to myself, I lost my job, but at least I can build a future with this man.

I was visiting my aunt Chris in New York soon after I lost my job. But at the time, I still had a boyfriend who promised the idea of marriage. My aunt and I were browsing through an old bookstore near Union Square. Somewhere between the "Staff's Favorite Selections" and the autobiography section, Aunt Chris turned to me and asked me how my job search was going. I told her that it was kind of slow, but that I hoped to be planning a wedding soon. She reached for my hand, picked it up, and told me that she didn't see a ring on my finger. She then said, "You need to focus on you and your goals. Put yourself first. Don't make plans waiting on someone else." My aunt had a good point. I was planning my future around someone who only proposed an idea of marriage, not an actual proposal. I was putting my future on hold waiting for someone else to make up his mind about our future together. Just because I lost my job didn't mean that I needed to lose my sense of independence.

Soon after my aunt's lecture on being independent, I was on my own again. My boyfriend broke off our relationship. He said that he changed his mind and didn't want to be with me. In that moment, I felt crushed. But the truth is I wasn't happy with him. And I didn't really love him. Breakups happen. People change their minds. Sometimes relationships don't work out. People grow in different directions. But it can still feel like a punch in the gut. And the timing of this breakup was awful. Work dumped me. A friend dumped me. And now my boyfriend was dumping me. I was feeling very rejected at this point. And it was only the third week of my big fall. At the time, I didn't know that I had two more bad weeks to go.

WEEK FOUR of my big fall. I recall from conversations that I had with my ex-boyfriend that he participated in risky behavior during his life. As a former reporter, I tend to ask a lot of questions. And as I entered into a committed relationship, I felt justified in asking personal questions about his past. It's not necessary for me to tell the specifics of his private information, but it became clear to me that my ex made some unsafe decisions before he met me. While I remember that he assured me that he was healthy and disease free, I no longer trusted everything that he said. I found it important, for my own peace of mind, to visit my OB/GYN and have a physical, including blood work. It was one of the most humiliating moments of my life. I'm a self-proclaimed germaphobe. I'm careful about what I put into my body. And my health is a priority. I dated a man I trusted. And now I had to question whether or not he was trustworthy. The responsible decision for me was to run some tests. Including an HIV test. This was a moment when I definitely said, "I never thought this would happen to me."

Waiting for my HIV results was one of the scariest times in my life because I knew it could be life changing. While I waited, I made "God Promises." You know what those are. *God, if you get me out of this, I promise to do (fill in the blank).* I was making God Promises. Lots of them. I was crying. I was worrying. I didn't sleep. I wondered how my life might change if I didn't get the results I was hoping for. I was on my knees praying. God delivered. My results showed that I had a clean, healthy body. It was one of the most thankful moments in my life. Yet still the home stretch of my big fall was coming. And it called for more God Promises.

WEEK FIVE of my really big fall. I had a lump on my back. Yes, the kind of lump that shouldn't be there. The kind of lump that continued to get bigger over time. The kind of lump that was out of sight. Out of sight, out of mind. I ignored my lump for over a year. My mom noticed it one day when I had my long hair pulled up in a ponytail. When others saw my back, it was easy to notice the huge mass next to my upper spine. It needed to come out. But what *exactly* was lying beneath my skin? Was it cancer? Was it something that I needed to worry about? Remember, I had no job. Which meant I had no health insurance. Those two facts were staring me in the face. While my lump was staring others in the face. I needed to get the lump off my back. I scheduled a surgery and had the mass removed. My lump was sent to pathology for testing. I got a call from my doctor when the results came in. I was going to be fine. It was not cancer. Another prayer answered by God. But it was time for me to heal. Time to heal the scar on my back. And the scars below the surface. I had collected many scars over time. And they all surfaced over my five-week free fall.

Scars. We all have them. And many of them are hidden. These are the scars that people can only see when we let them. They come from the battles we fight when we're at our lowest of lows. They are the scars that come from the embarrassment of a job loss. Or working for an unpleasant boss. They are the scars that come from toxic relationships. Or from people who abuse us mentally or physically. They are the scars that come from trusting someone who betrays you after you've shared your soul with him or her. They are the scars that come from battling an illness and fighting to save your own life. They are the scars that come from losing someone you love. We get these scars and wounds during the battles of life. And these battles can take us through a long, steep climb. And just when we get to the top, the law of gravity kicks in. And we fall. But we have to get back up.

You work hard at your job and show that you're a dedicated employee. You put your time into a company and climb the corporate ladder. And then after years of loyalty, you lose your job. You worked your way up. And then you come crashing down. You are loyal and true in your relationships. You take the time to nurture the relationships, cultivate trust in the relationships, and give your heart to the relationships. And then the trust is broken. You come crashing down from the pain of heartbreak. You take care of your body. You live the life of a healthy person. You eat well. You exercise. You treat your body like the temple that it is. And then you're diagnosed with a life-changing disease. You feel your world come crashing down. But what goes up, must come down. It's a fact of life. So how do you climb back up after a fall? It's true what they say...one day at a time.

After my five-week fall, I felt pretty low. I lost confidence in myself and trust in others. I didn't feel motivated to do much of anything. And I just had surgery on my back, so intense workouts to vent off steam were out of the question. But my legs worked. And I could still walk and breathe. I was jobless, boyfriendless, and scarred. But I was still alive. A lot happened in five short weeks. And it started a time of great reflection for me. When you go through painful times, it's a good time to reflect on what you've been through and where you want to go. You can mourn the past, but know that there is still a future. It's a great time to enjoy your own company. You can start a new climb. And remember, every time you fall, you must always get back up.

six

Live Your Walk Out Song

Playlist Song: "Stronger" Kelly Clarkson

What is your walk out song? For those who don't know, your walk out song is your theme song. It's a song that can change many times in your lifetime. It may be a song that expresses your fun and flirty mood. I once chose "Cherry Pie" by Warrant as my fun walk out song. It doesn't really have the full effect without fans blowing your hair around like an eighties music video. And who walks around with full-powered fans? But there was a time when I had big hair, wore frosted pink lipstick, and should have purchased stock in Aqua Net aerosol hair spray. I still feel nostalgic when I hear eighties music like "Cherry Pie."

And then there was the song that I chose after a close friend blindsided me with a hurtful betrayal. I played Christina Aguilera's "Fighter" over and over again. In fact, I rocked out to that song many times in my car and on the treadmill. And of course we all have a song that we play once we reach the anger phase after a bad breakup. Mine was "Fuck You" by Lily Allen. The lyrics of the song don't apply to my breakup, but I loved the way Allen gleefully sings the words "fuck you," as if to sound sweet with a smile on her face. As it relates to this chapter, your walk out song symbolizes taking your power back from a painful experience. Much of what I write about in this chapter specifically speaks to women. I've had so many conversations with men over the years who complain about the women in their lives and the so-called "crazy" things they do. Many of these women are smart, beautiful, successful, and kind women. But the truth is we all have a little bit of crazy in us if our buttons are pushed. When I listened to the stories that these men told about women, I wanted to defend the women and give them some advice. And truthfully, I could listen to my own advice from time to time. So ladies...this is what I would say to you and to me as you're living your walk out song...

STOP YOUR CRAZY! It's a phrase my girlfriend and I say to each other every time our emotions start to act up over a guy. You know you've done it. In fact, you know when you're doing it. It's almost like an out-of-body experience. You can see that it's *you* acting crazy. You can hear that it's *your* voice sounding crazy. But you just can't seem to stop yourself from acting like a crazy bitch. It's not how you want to act. But some guy comes along and hurts your feelings so badly that your crazy emotions take over your body. Dare I write the craziest thing I ever did? In the spirit of honesty, I will. I was arguing with a guy I was dating. It was a battle of who can yell the loudest and make the least amount of sense. I can't even recall what we were arguing about, but I'm quite certain I made no sense at all. We were arguing in his car, in my driveway, and he wanted to leave. *What?!* He was going to drive away from me when this argument (whatever it was that I can't remember) was still unresolved? The crazy person that possessed my body in that moment stormed out of the car, left the door wide open, and jumped on the front hood of his car! Oh yes I did. I threw my body on a hunk of metal as if to say, *Try leaving me now!* I'm sure my mother will be mortified when she reads this. It was not a shining moment in my past. And my mom raised me to be more of a lady than my apparent She-Ra self. Reflecting on that moment, I'm embarrassed just thinking about it. I was in my early twenties, but that's no excuse. I threw my body on a car! Who does that? Yep, a crazy person! If you've been in a bad relationship, you've probably buried an embarrassing moment deep in your memory bank. If I could handle that moment differently, I would give myself some advice: Before you go on a crazy binge, call your best girlfriend and make sure she tells you to STOP YOUR CRAZY! Acting crazy will never win a guy over. Nor will it win him back. And if he happens to be the kind of guy who likes his women a little crazy, you don't want him. Letting your emotions get out of control is not good for your health or your psyche. And it's certainly not good for your pride. When someone hurts you to the point of making you crazy, it's time to walk away and release him or her from your life.

HIT "PAUSE" ON THE RIFLE CALLING. I never heard the phrase "rifle call" until I did it. It's when you rapidly speed dial someone over and over again. It's when you make a record number of calls in sixty seconds. I think my personal best was something like fourteen calls in one minute. I'm sure our grandparents and parents never rifle called. That was the one good thing about rotary phones...they took too long to dial a number. But in an age where you only have to hit one button to call a number, rifle calling is way too tempting to a person who is mad as hell on the other line. Rifle calls are rarely answered. And these calls are certainly unwanted by the person you're dialing. In fact, the person you're calling is most likely avoiding you. Let's turn the table around. If someone called you multiple times in five minutes, would you want to answer his or her call? I would venture to say probably not. Not only is it annoying, but it's embarrassing. Why would you try calling someone multiple times who doesn't want to talk to you? If it's to create a sense of urgency, you're better off sending an urgent text message. And then waiting for a response. So when you get the urge to dial a phone number at rapid pace, stop yourself. However you do it, you must hit "pause" on your rifle calling!

Don't be a victim of the PUSH AND PULL SYNDROME. Have you found yourself repeatedly saying, in a begging tone, "When am I going to see you again?" or "I feel like you never want to spend time with me anymore," or "I feel like you don't make me a priority." Statements that revolve around these feelings are a sign that there's been a shift in your relationship. While I know I have some real-life adult examples of this, let me tell you the story of when I first learned about the push and pull syndrome. It was in the first grade. One of the cutest boys in the class sat in front of me. His name was Jeff. He was a little bit shorter than me and had beautiful blond hair and long, dark eyelashes. All of the girls in the class had a crush on him. One day, between spelling and math class, I asked Jeff, "What girls do you like best in school?" Jeff replied, "You, Nikki, and Jennifer." I smiled and felt happy that my name was on that list. After I stared at the back of his blond head for a few minutes, I decided to tap Jeff on the shoulder and ask him again, "What girls do you like best in school?" He smiled and repeated his first answer, "You, Nikki, and Jennifer." For some reason, I felt thrilled that his answer had not changed in five minutes. I sat through a forty-five-minute math class and watched the clock tick before I had the chance to talk to Jeff again. And then, as if I hadn't fully understood his answer the first two times, I persisted by asking Jeff a third time, "What girls do you like best in school?" He took a deep sigh, and as aggravated as a six-year-old boy can be, he responded, "Nikki and Jennifer!"

I was off the list! It's an elementary example, but I was still pushing for an answer, which made the boy pull away. When you push yourself on someone too much, they will pull away. If it's someone who deserves your heart and attention, you won't have to push. He will want to be with you. He will make time for you. And if he doesn't, he doesn't really want you. If you find yourself begging for someone's time and attention, stop. You are demeaning yourself when you beg someone to spend time with you. You are devaluing your own worth. No guy, girl, man, or woman is worth begging to stay. Stop groveling. Pick yourself up off the floor. Brush off your pride. Shoulders back. Head held high. And walk away. Don't look back. Maybe he'll come after you. Maybe he won't. But let the decision to walk away be your decision. In the end, you'll feel so much better about yourself. And if he leaves you, he did you a favor. Time is precious. No sense in wasting it on a game of push and pull. You'll never get anywhere when you play that game.

TRUST YOUR GUT on everything! I'm a firm believer that your gut is your brain's way of giving you a fact. It may not be a fact that you can see with your own eyes. But I believe it's a fact that your instincts know to be true. Now if you're an extremely paranoid person, this section may not apply to you. But for those of us who have a level head about life, trust your gut. If you think he's cheating, he probably is. If you sense that he's lying, you're probably right. If your gut tells you that he's going to end up being no good for you, your gut is speaking the truth. So often we talk ourselves out of what our gut is telling us.

I remember meeting a guy who I thought was Mr. Perfect. He had a great job, his family was awesome, he was handsome, we liked all of the same things, and he was really into me. But every time I was with him, something didn't feel right. I couldn't put my finger on what it was. Instead of following my intuition, I ignored my gut instinct. He was the kind of guy who said all of the right things. He delivered his words with conviction. But something inside of me felt he was being dishonest. I had no proof that he was dishonest, but something didn't feel right about him.

I ignored my gut and talked myself into believing in all of the good qualities that he represented. I should have trusted my gut. This guy turned out to be a con man with a secret past that he was hiding. He didn't fool my gut. But I let him fool me.

We say things like, "He's different with me..."; "You don't know him the way that I do..."; "I think he's changed..."; "I must be overthinking things..." We feed our minds with excuses. We want to wish away bad information. And we think if we wish it away, it won't be true. We create a vision in our minds about how we want things to be. And sometimes we allow that vision to be our reality when it is not. If you allow yourself to see things clearly, you cannot ignore facts. You cannot ignore your gut. It will rarely let you down.

STOP FACEBOOK STALKING! You know you've done it. You're hung up on your ex, someone who rejected you, or some-one you wished liked you. And you look at his or her Facebook page one hundred times a day. Okay, maybe it's less than that. Maybe it's more?

One afternoon, I text messaged my girlfriend and told her that I was feeling weak. She knew I didn't mean that I had low energy. It was clear to my friend that I was feeling sad about a guy. Her response was, "You will get past this. Do not text him or Facebook stalk his page!"

I knew that I was smart, polished, and desirable. But this guy who rejected me made me feel so undesirable. After I prom-ised my friend that I would not Facebook stalk the guy who rejected me, I thought about other women who felt rejected in their lives. I wondered if Facebook stalking had any boundaries based on a woman's level of desirability. So I asked my friend, "Do you think that Jennifer Aniston ever stalked anyone on Facebook?" I suppose that somehow I wanted to think that all women, even one of the most appealing stars in Hollywood, have weak moments. I met Jennifer Aniston once. She was the total package...beautiful, fit, funny, friendly, smart, and successful. I wondered if a girl who seemed to have everything also had insecurities over men. My friend's response to that question was, "How would you feel if you had to look at pictures of your ex plastered everywhere with Angelina Jolie?"

I got her point. It doesn't matter how beautiful, famous, rich, or desirable you are...everyone has a weak moment when he or she is rejected. But trust me, social media stalking will just prolong your recovery if you're trying to get over an ex. Delete your ex. Block your ex. Just please, stop social media stalking your ex!

My friend and I then talked about how classy Jennifer Aniston remained in the public eye after her breakup with Brad Pitt. I have no idea how she felt privately, but as women, I think we can all identify with the feelings associated with love, loss, and heartbreak. This Hollywood star was a great example of demonstrating poise and grace during a very public breakup. Which leads me to my next piece of good advice...

KEEP YOUR CLASS INTACT...or at least fake it (God knows, it's not the only thing women fake). This one can be tough. In the song "Before He Cheats," Carrie Underwood sings about wanting to take a Louisville slugger to a car's headlights after the man in her song wrongs her. I think a lot of women can identify with that feeling. Whether you want to smash his car, smack him in the face, or F-bomb him as if it's the only word in the dictionary...STOP! Take a long, deep breath before you do any of it. It may feel like a good idea in the moment to do physical or verbal damage to the offender. But that moment will pass. And you may end up regretting what you've said or done. I prefer to side with class rather than trash. Maybe you're thinking to yourself, "Why do I have to be the better person?" Maybe you're thinking that he deserves a taste of his own medicine. But you deserve more! Don't let your volatile emotions about a guy be a reflection of you. They won't have the impact that you're hoping for. When you scream, swear, and throw a tantrum, you lose pieces of yourself. You may feel like an explosion of fireworks on the inside, but let your outer self stay classy. Women have the great gift of being able to fake it when necessary. You may not feel like acting classy, but it takes strength of character to look someone in the eye, tell him that the relationship isn't working for you anymore, and walk away. Be a lady. Be classy. You'll be thankful that you were.

TAKE YOUR POWER BACK. How the heck are you supposed to do this when you gave it away? It's possible. And you can. The secret is that you control your power. It's simple to explain how you gave it away. You cry over him. You beg him to come back. You keep asking, "Why don't you love me?" And you sorrowfully tell him, "I don't understand why you don't want to be with me." You remind him of all the promises he made to you, even though he's changed his mind. You show up at the places you know he'll be just to see him. You drop everything for him even though he's blown you off for months or longer. You are like a puppet on a string. You move and turn every way that he wants you to. You are predictable to him. And you feel you've lost control of yourself when it comes to him. He has power over you because you gave it to him. So let's change that.

First let me say that if you're in an abusive relationship, you should seek out professional help. You should always protect yourself. Find a person or organization who can help you. For all other relationships gone bad, here are some thoughts on how to take your power back. Hit the "restart" button on your emotions. If you think that you got too emotional during your last interaction, consider having one more quick exchange that is upbeat and professional. This exchange can be in person or on the phone. Make it short and sweet. And to the point. Do not get emotional. Do not ask personal questions. And if this exchange happens in person, make sure you look really good! When we look good on the outside, we feel even better on the inside. And when we feel good on the inside, our confidence comes pouring out. It doesn't really matter that he thinks you look good. What matters is that you see yourself as looking good.

Allow this final exchange to be your own personal closure. Your phone calls and text messages have to stop. Even though it's hard, do not respond to him. There is nothing more to say. If you speak to him while you're feeling weak, then you are empowering him. The only way to fully take your power back from someone who mistreated you is to cut him out of your life. It will be hard. You will miss him. You will want to call him. You will want to see him. You will think of him when a certain song comes on the radio. You will remember the happy times when you visit a location that was "your place." But it's time for you to close that chapter in your life.

And finally, the most important part of taking your power back is to make yourself the number one priority in your life. Focus on you. Put your energy into doing things that make you happy and fulfilled. Find a new hobby or pick up an old one. Become reacquainted with yourself and the things that bring pleasure into your life. Enjoy your own company and the company of positive people. It's time to make new memories. It's time to open yourself up to new possibilities. And if you want to live your playlist, maybe it's time to choose your walk out song. It may be a cliché, but it's true that what doesn't kill you makes you stronger. So stand tall. Be strong. Focus on you. Take your power back. And walk out with your head held high.

seven

Fine-Tune Your People Picker

Playlist Song & Artist: "Fighter" Christina Aguilera

Betrayals hurt. You can only be betrayed by people you trust. It's painful when people you trust turn their back on you because you chose to trust them and they did not honor that trust. This was the premise of a conversation I was having with my brother, Paul, one summer afternoon. We were sipping his homemade Moscow mules. The taste of ginger beer, fresh mint, and vodka was refreshing on a day when something heavy was weighing on my mind. I caught my brother at a time when he was free to ponder the complexities of life. And the effects of his homemade cocktails made our analysis of human behavior seem brilliant that afternoon! At least it did to us. Paul is my younger brother in age. But at six feet four inches he stands eight inches taller and sturdier than me. Sometimes I think his stature makes him seem wiser than me too. My visit came on the heels of a painful betrayal from a friend I trusted for many years. And I couldn't put my finger on what went wrong. I was under the impression that this friend placed value on our friendship. And it was a friendship that had a special place in my heart. I allowed myself to be raw and vulnerable in front of this friend over the years. I'm sure you've had this kind of friend. He or she is the person with whom you choose to share your demons. And you feel comfortable sharing your most personal thoughts with this person because you believe that he or she will never judge, betray, or turn his or her back on you. You place this person on a friendship pedestal. And you're happy to tell anyone who will listen about your amazing friend and the positive influence he or she has on your life. This is your go-to friend. Your confidante. Your rock. But what do you do when that friend lets you down in a hurtful way? How do you handle the moment when you realize that your friend is not a friend at all? The answer seems simple. You end the friendship. But betrayals are never that easy. And ending a friendship can be a difficult process and a sad experience.

My friendship in question was one that was tested in good and bad times. But through our highs and lows, we always seemed to remain close. We shared private details of our lives with each other. We talked almost every day. And we became entrenched in each other's lives. We supported each other through many of life's challenges. But she turned her back on me when I needed her most. My career was in turmoil and my personal life was in shambles. I hit a low point in my life. I needed the love and encouraging words of my friend while I mourned my losses. Maybe my struggles were too much for her? Maybe she never cared about me? Maybe I placed more value on the friendship than she did? But I do know that she said some hurtful words to me as she ended our friendship. And she shared some of our private conversations with others. It became clear that my supposed friend didn't think highly of me at all. I was left stunned. I felt as though I let this friend read my private diary. And then she blasted and burned every page that

I wrote. This person I once held close as a trusted friend left me feeling as if I was standing alone and exposed.

I shared every detail of the fallen friendship with my brother. Including my play-by-play analysis on the betrayal. He listened closely. Shaking his head at appropriate times. All while enjoying his Moscow mule, out of a copper cup, in the comfort of his Cape Cod-style kitchen. When I finished my long story, my brother offered some simple advice. He told me that I needed to fine-tune my people picker.

My people picker was off. I was allowing unworthy people into my inner circle. My recent story of betrayal had a common theme when I examined it closely. I was making mistakes that many of us make. I trusted people too quickly. I shared too much of my life before real trust was earned. I was an over-sharer. And in the process, I was overlooking the warning signs that a good people picker would pick up on. When I examined my "friendships-gone-bad," I recognized that these were often people who were fast friends. Meaning we became too close too fast. We spent copious amounts of time talking. And we shared personal information too quickly. It wasn't a slow bonding process. It was like speed dating for a new friend. This is not a good idea. Trust takes time to build. Building strong friendships should be a slow and careful process. It should take time to get to know the depth of someone. Be cautious about anyone who wants to share too much or know your life story before all four seasons have passed.

I also recognized that many of the bad friends I allowed into my life often had trouble maintaining solid friendships. This is an obvious warning sign. If people can't keep quality friends in their lives, then they probably won't keep you around either. You should also be wary of people who have too much drama in their lives. It's way too easy to get sucked into the soap opera story lines of other people's lives. Eventually the negativity and exhaustion of their drama will pull you down and prevent you from enjoying healthy relationships. Drama can be contagious. Protect yourself from that emotional disease. It seems obvious that these are all characteristics of a bad friend. But sometimes people can pull a sneak attack on you. They appear to be one type of person and then, just when you're not looking, you're attacked or hurt by the person you thought was your friend. And sometimes we create people who are much better in our minds than they are in real life. Our blinders are on. Our people picker is off. We want to believe the best in people we let into our lives. And we ignore the warning signs of an unworthy friend.

After working in the television industry for almost twenty years and then leaving the airwaves, I quickly found out who liked me because they liked *me*. And sadly, I discovered that some people only liked me because I was "the girl on TV." I found that as my circle of friends became tighter, many of my true friends were people I had known for years. I shared a history with these friends. Sometimes we need to reflect on why we chose old friends to remember what it takes to have long-lasting friendships. As I reflected on my longtime friendships, I saw examples of when I had a good people picker. While these examples pay tribute to important friends in my life, I hope you'll recognize that these people represent the characteristics of someone special in your life.

I'm not sure that I would be the person I am today without my amazing friend Lori. We met when I was a kid intern working for a television talk show. She was a brilliant psychologist who appeared as a regular guest on the show. Lori always came dressed in professional suits with a sexy twist. She was the TV psychologist all the men in the studio drooled over, but who seemed unaware of her sex appeal. Lori is funny, sharp, quick witted, and always draws a captive audience when she speaks. When I first spent time talking to Lori, I knew she would make a good friend. Luckily for me, she wanted to be my friend too. We got together for monthly lunches. At first we talked about television and simple stories happening in our lives. But eventually those simple stories developed into more meaningful conversations about our triumphs and setbacks in life.

Over the span of a twenty-year friendship, Lori got to know the depth of me. It was a testament to our years of friendship. I could be raw and vulnerable in front of her. And I knew that I would never be judged. I felt secure knowing that Lori would never turn her back on me. And she always championed me as I searched for true happiness and fulfillment. Lori talked me through my darkest moments and challenged me to become wiser through my life experiences. I could never cry too many tears, whine too often, or worry too much in front of my longtime friend. I'm sure I sounded like a broken record at times. Bitching, complaining, and crying about the same struggles. But my friend never lost her patience with me. Lori allowed me to work through my emotions at my own pace. And she guided me to find answers to my own questions. Lori helped me find my voice when I was afraid to speak. She helped me clear my thoughts when I didn't understand what I was thinking. And she helped me find peace in my life. She is the reason I found the courage to write this book. And she believed that I had stories to tell and pass on to others. Consider yourself a blessed person if you have a friend who knows the depth of you, who considers it an honor to have your friendship, and who thinks you are even more beautiful because you are flawed. I found all of these qualities in my devoted friend Lori.

When I think of a friend who makes me laugh uncontrollably, I think of my friend Melody. We met when we were in our twenties. Melody is a beautiful married soccer mom who always carries Prada and Gucci bags, but often brags about the $20 jeans she finds on sale at Marshall's. She prides herself on trying to be frugal. I was single when we met. I didn't own any Prada bags. And I was trying to date her brother-in-law. It didn't work out with her brother-in-law, but I gained a wonderful friend in the process. Melody and I were raised in very different homes. My parents were always around, and I didn't have to want for anything. Whereas Melody had to work for everything. Melody was raised by her grandparents after she lost her mother to a brutal crime at the age of nine. I can't imagine what it would be like to grow up without a mother, as my mom played a vital role in my development as a woman. But when I observe my friend Melody, she teaches me about the importance of being resilient. This woman faced many challenges in her life. But she never complained. She never placed blame. And she always found a positive spin on everything. Melody is the friend who cried with me the moment I lost my job and who made me laugh in the same conversation at the absurdity of wearing Jimmy Choo shoes in the unemployment line. (I didn't own a Prada bag, but I did have Jimmy Choo shoes that my mother gave me. They were my one coveted pair of shoes because I could never afford to buy my own.) Whenever I felt sad or lonely, Melody and her family welcomed me into their home, poured me a drink, and reminded me that time with good friends helps to push the "pause" button on life's struggles. And sometimes we just need a few hours to hit "pause" on life.

When I struggled, Melody told me that I was beautiful, smart, and talented. She made me feel I was a prize to be won, both personally and professionally. I always left our conversations with my head held high and smiling. We all need a friend who can make us laugh, even during difficult times. And it's even better to have a friend who can make us feel fabulous when we feel anything but that about ourselves.

I made one of my best friends in life at work. And while I think it's good to separate your work life from your personal life, I'm so thankful that I met my friend Diana. We first met when we were working for the same employer who eventually fired me. I was the new girl. Diana was a veteran in the business.

I was dating a guy who wasn't treating me well. One night, while my boyfriend at the time was pulling his usual shenanigans, Diana gave him a piece of her mind and publicly stood up for me. Diana defended me, and we weren't even good friends at the time. I knew after that incident she was the kind of person I wanted as a friend. Diana stands about six inches shorter than me, but her personality owns the room. My feisty Irish-Italian friend with fair skin and long, black, curly hair is a woman I would do battle next to any day of the week. Diana is a woman I admire for her professional success but love for her extreme loyalty. Some might say she is loyal to a fault. I don't think loyalty has faults. And I've been blessed to have her loyalty from the moment she chewed out the boy I was dating. Diana took me to dinner regularly during my "professional hiatus." She talked to me about my professional strengths and encouraged me to look for work in areas where I would flourish. Diana always championed my successes and tried to guide me through my setbacks. When I was jobless and felt weak, she reminded me of my talents. In fact, Diana created a position for me with her company while I tried to figure out my next career move. She offered me something that I longed for through the position she created. Diana put me in an environment where I was valued, treated like a true professional, and able to learn from others what it means to be a great leader. Her friendship helped keep my confidence intact at a time when my confidence was wavering. It takes a special friend to make you believe that you have value in this world when you question your own value. Find a friend who reminds you of your value.

One of the most valued people in my life is my friend Dominique. I first met Dominique when I was interviewing her for a charity event that she was promoting on my television show. Dominique is an Olympic gold medalist. And while her tiny frame once stood on a podium wearing a gold medal around her neck, it's her spirit that is worth its weight in gold.

I remember watching Dominique compete on television when she was a young girl. I was just a teenager at that time and had no idea that the young gymnast representing the USA would someday became one of my most valued friends. Dominique is a woman I connected with the moment I met her. I could immediately sense her good soul. But our friendship took its time to evolve. At the beginning of our new friendship, we met for lunches and talked about our work lives and families. Over time, as trust was built, we talked more about our dreams and goals for the future. These conversations included personal setbacks and triumphs that happened in our lives. Dominique has a strong moral compass and places great value on being honest and true to your word. If Dominique says she's going to do something, she follows through on her commitment.

As I observed Dominique's dedication to commitment, I was challenged to be more like her. She also inspired me to remain positive when facing immense hurdles. I receive weekly text messages in the form of inspirational quotes from Dominique that remind me of my goals and dreams. Dominique tackles every dream in her life with full force. She makes no exceptions. Dominique believes in everything that she sets her sights on. And if my friend faces a roadblock, she finds a way to rise above it. Dominique has unshakeable courage and faith. And throughout the course of our friendship, I always hoped that her qualities would become infectious. I observed her. I listened to her. I learned from her. And I became a better person for knowing her. Faith and courage...what beautiful gifts to receive from a beautiful friend.

When I reflect on these key friendships, I notice a common theme. These friendships saw many seasons together, year after year. And our friendships were unwavering throughout that time. Friendships can be tested. These friendships never failed me. And these women were always by my side. No matter what. They are all smart and funny, successful and nurturing, honest and kind. Their backgrounds are all different. And they all lived through their own sets of challenges, which brought substance and wisdom to their lives. They are selfless friends who never fight with me. They never make me feel bad about myself. They never judge me. And they don't criticize me. When I need to vent about something multiple times, they let me. And when I finally put my whining to rest, they celebrate with me. My people picker was spot-on when I chose to bring these friends into my life. We support each other. We challenge each other. We have thought-provoking conversations with each other. But we also know how to be silly and laugh unguardedly with each other. When I spend time with these friends, my heart feels happy. And they nourish my soul. None of these friends come with bad reputations. And they don't have questionable qualities that I need to overlook. These four women have something very important in common. They all have good hearts. I knew their hearts would never be selfish and never betray me. When you have friends like this in your life, they should be the standard to which you hold up all other potential friends who come along.

When I reflected on the friends who betrayed my trust over the years, I recognized that they didn't have the qualities of these key friends. But I also learned that bad friends can be a good thing. There is a lesson in betrayal. You must look for the takeaway when it happens to you. Hurtful friendships will help you fine-tune your people picker. If you notice a pattern when you are betrayed, recognize the pattern and break the pattern. Be sure to give a friendship time to develop. Its true identity will reveal itself in time. People can't hide what they truly are. Take time before you allow a friend inside your heart and soul. That is a lesson I learned the hard way. There's no rush to reveal all of your pains and grievances right away. Be cautious of those who say "you can trust me" over and over again. There is truth in the theory that thou doth protest too much. Never trust an adult friend who asks you to "pinky swear." Yes, this happened to me. And since I was too old to be wearing bows in my hair, it always made me uncomfortable when a grown person held out her pinky finger for me to make a promise. It's a childish line and should only be reserved for third graders (and I didn't even do it in third grade). Do more listening than you do talking before you decide to trust someone with your friendship. When you listen, you'll hear what kind of people they are, how they treat other friends, and how they view their friendships. And when someone hurts you or betrays you, and this will happen, feel good about saying good-bye to the friendship. Not all people are meant to stay in your life forever. You can be grateful for the good times you had and thankful that you no longer have someone toxic in your life.

When I was struggling with the betrayal of a person I thought was a friend, I turned on my playlist and went for a good run while listening to "Fighter" by Christina Aguilera. It's the perfect song to listen to after someone you trust hurts you. Christina sings the words with passion, and I think the emotion in the music is universal for all people who feel that they've been burned by someone they loved. Betrayals start with hurt, which turns into anger. But as time passes, the message in the song "Fighter" is true. You become wiser. You become stronger. And you become thankful for the lessons you learned from those who hurt you. It's one of the great lessons I learned while living my playlist.

eight

Be the Lead Actor in Your Life

Playlist Song & Artist: "Work Bitch" Britney Spears

While I was working as a talk show host in Cleveland, I had some of the most amazing opportunities come my way. When I was younger, I used to think these opportunities happened because of pure luck. But now I realize that while luck plays a small role, great opportunities happen because of hard work, drive, focusing on your goals, and developing strong relationships. Not the kind of relationship where you kiss someone's ass or put on a phony persona just to get what you want. That never came naturally to me. I believe in building relationships with people because you truly like them or because it feels good to help someone without expecting anything in return. But somewhere, somehow, a show of gratitude is usually returned when you do something nice for another person. I've been the recipient of gratitude many times in my life. But one specific show of gratitude taught me how to be the leading lady in my life.

While working in television, I met a friend of a friend who was coming to Cleveland for the filming of Marvel's *The Avengers*. The movie studio chose Cleveland as one of its

102

filming locations for some of the action scenes. Cleveland was all abuzz about the filming of a huge superhero movie in town! And of course most Clevelanders hoped that our city would make a great impression on the film's cast and crew. I was asked to show one of the crew members around town. It was his first visit to Cleveland. I was a huge movie buff and thought it would be fun to meet someone in the film industry. Plus, I loved introducing newcomers to hot spots and hidden gems around town. I immediately started making plans to show off Cleveland to my unknown Los Angeles visitor.

Cleveland often got a bad rap from people who were unfamiliar with the city. In fact, when I was on a trip to New Orleans (a city that I love), I was taking a bus tour of the Big Easy. Somewhere between New Orleans's famous graveyards and one of Emeril's restaurants, the tour guide quoted American writer Tennessee Williams. The quote was "America has only three cities: New York, San Francisco, and New Orleans. Everywhere else is Cleveland." Dissed by Tennessee Williams! My friend sitting next to me on the bus started laughing while I began defending my hometown. After I politely debated the quote with the friendly tour guide, who had never visited Cleveland, I reminded myself that it was a dead playwright's thoughts and not the opinion of the woman giving the bus tour. That was the only moment during my New Orleans trip that I rolled my eyes in annoyance. The reason I tell that story is because Cleveland is often criticized by people who have never visited the city. I was determined to show my soon-to-be Hollywood friend that Cleveland wasn't just "everywhere else."

Little did I know that when I met Barry from Marvel Studios, he would not only become a friend, but he would also give me the opportunity of a lifetime! I was about to learn the value of becoming the lead actor in my life. Prior to his arrival in

Cleveland, Barry and I exchanged a few introductory e-mails so that our initial meeting wouldn't seem awkward. Through our e-mail exchange, I made plans with Barry to show him around Cleveland during a day off from filming. I tried to get a feel for the type of food and atmosphere he liked, and from there, I put a solid plan together to hit a few of the best spots in town.

First I took my new friend to a restaurant where the short ribs melt in your mouth. I knew Cleveland could win over any visitor with great food! My friend Rocco Whalen, who owns a restaurant called Fahrenheit, creates melt-in-your-mouth short ribs. This dish is fail proof and a must try for any meat eater! After dinner, I included some sight-seeing as a part of my tour. Around the corner from Fahrenheit sits a beautiful Russian Orthodox cathedral where Robert De Niro shot scenes for the movie *Deer Hunter*. I thought this church would make an interesting stop for a guy who makes movies for a living. During our tour, I found out that my new West Coast friend loves good beer. A trip to the Cleveland brew institution, Great Lakes Brewing Company, was a must! Known for their Burning River Pale Ale, Dortmunder Gold, and seasonal Christmas Ale, this brewery in the historic Ohio City district is worth a visit for any beer lover.

From the brewing company, we traveled to another popular downtown spot where the rooftop drinks at a certified green restaurant called the Greenhouse Tavern come with a great view of the busy street below. On our way to the rooftop bar, we passed celebrity chef Michael Symon's restaurant, Lola, and saw a group of men waving at us from their table through the restaurant window. Barry and I both waved back, even though I thought the waves were meant for me. I smiled at the group of men and offered an exaggerated wave even though I couldn't make out their faces through the window. I assumed that because this was my city, the men couldn't possibly know the stranger walking next to me. I decided that they must be friends or fans of my television show. It turns out I was wrong.

Immediately Barry turned to me and said, "That's Joss Wheeden, the director of *The Avengers,* and some of the producers from the movie. Come on, I want to introduce you to them." He grabbed my hand and pulled me toward the restaurant where the director and producers were dining.

Barry and I walked into the sleek restaurant and over to the table where the Hollywood heavyweights were dining. The group didn't seem to mind our intrusion. We exchanged some laughs and easy conversation. Before we left the table, Barry and I invited the group to join us at the rooftop bar next door. They agreed to swing by. At some point in the night, I think the entire crew from *The Avengers* joined us for some rooftop socializing.

As the night progressed, Barry turned to me and said, "Now that you've met the director, let's try to get you on set for an interview." Scheduling a set visit and an interview with someone from *The Avengers* was something that every journalist in town coveted. While the idea of being the first journalist to visit *The Avengers* set was exciting to me, I just wanted to enjoy the moment and my new company. I was in my glory on a rooftop full of moviemakers!

Over the next couple of weeks, Barry brought me onto *The Avengers* set to watch the filmmaking process. I didn't come with a camera. And I didn't Tweet or Facebook about the scenes I was watching. I wanted to be respectful of the secrecy of the film's content. And understandably, Marvel Studios was very protective about the content of their movie that was in production. I was in awe of the million-dollar set that I visited. I quietly watched the filmmaking process. Fifty feet from where I was standing, I watched the evil character Loki, played by actor Tom Hiddleston, battle actor Chris Evans, who played Captain America. And I sat wide-eyed as a stuntman was thrown from a high window onto a cab, with real blood running down his face from an action scene. It was my first time on a movie set! Every sight and sound ignited the same kind of excitement that kids feel when they still believe in Santa Claus on Christmas morning. For years I reviewed films, but this was the first time that I watched the making of a movie. It was surreal. And it gave me goose bumps.

And then one day, while filming was still taking place, Barry gave me some news that I wasn't expecting in a million years. In fact, it was a thought that never crossed my mind. In a drawn-out, yet trying-to-disguise-his-excitement tone, Barry told me that I would not be able to do an interview on the set of the movie. Instead, I was going to shoot a scene for the movie! He told me that it was arranged for me to play the role of a reporter in the film!

"How is this possible?" I thought. "I'm not an actress." My only acting experience was in Pioneer Theatre, a community theater group for kids in my hometown. I was around ten years old when I played the role of the spinning top in *The Velveteen Rabbit*. It was a small role, and I can still remember my one line, "Watch out, here I come!" And now, with nothing but the training of a community theater group, I was going to shoot a scene in *The Avengers*! *OH MY GOD!* You can imagine what the phone call to my family sounded like in the privacy of my own car. I could barely contain my excitement! And I still have the voice message that my sister, Kathleen, left me after she found out about my movie role. She was so excited that to this day I can't understand much of what she is saying in her message.

The day I was called onto the movie set to shoot my scene, I wasn't sure what to expect. When I showed up, I realized that I was the only person playing a reporter that day. I thought I would have one short line, maybe two. I didn't receive a script prior to filming, so I assumed that my line would be easy to memorize. One of the producers on set handed me a sheet of paper with paragraphs typed out. The paragraphs were titled *Reporter 1*, *Reporter 2*, *Reporter 3*, and so on through *Reporter 8*. The producer told me to pick two of the paragraphs and to let him know when I was ready to shoot my scene. He added that there was no pressure and to take my time to prepare.

What? No pressure?! I was on the set of an expected blockbuster movie, the director of the film was sitting right in front of me, I'm not an actress, and I wasn't supposed to be nervous?! I quickly pulled out my phone and started texting my biggest cheerleader. My mom. The exchange went something like this:

Me: "I'm on the set now. This is so cool! But I have many lines to say and I'm not an actress. I'm freaking out."

Mom: "You'll be great! Just deliver your lines with conviction."

Me: "I don't think I can do this."

Mom: "Yes you can! Believe that you can do it and you will."

Me: "But I'm not an actress."

Mom: "You're my daughter. I believe you can do it. It's time to be the lead actress in your life. Enjoy this moment and own it."

Me: "Okay, thanks, Mom. I better go. I have to start memorizing the paragraphs they gave me. This is so exciting!"

Mom: "Good luck! I can't wait to hear all about it."

The lead actress in my own life? It was an interesting thought. Especially now. In reality I was an extra on set with some speaking lines. But I knew what my mom meant. I needed to be the star of my own story line. And in that moment, my story line was a woman who had the opportunity of a lifetime to film a scene on the set of a huge movie. The part was small. But the role it played in my life was huge. I stared at my lines for the next forty-five minutes. Trying my best to memorize the words. I rallied myself and decided that the time to shoot my scene was now or never. I told the director that I was ready to film. Inside, I was a little uncertain of myself. But I dismissed the uncertainty. I reminded myself of that time, many years before, when I felt unsure of myself before the Russell Crowe interview. I owned the moment then. And I needed to own the moment now. It was time to take a leap of faith and pretend to be an actress for the day. It was time to be the lead actor in my life.

As I followed my cameraman and crew to my filming location, I made sure to take in the sights and sounds going on around me. I knew this kind of moment would never happen again. While I was waiting to shoot my scene, actor Chris Evans was shooting one of his scenes about twenty feet away from me. He was wearing his Captain America costume, and he definitely had a movie star aura around him. The lights were shining brightly upon Chris Evans. And even though he was wearing blue-and-red spandex, he looked gorgeous.

There were extras everywhere. They were all wearing torn and tattered clothing. The storefronts of the downtown buildings were converted into shattered glass with fake body parts on the streets and sidewalks. Taxi cabs were turned upside down and fake smoke was being pumped into the street. My scene was going to be shot in the middle of the created chaos. I wore a professional black dress that was covered with fake soot. Dust was sprinkled in my hair and wiped on my face by one of the makeup artists. I needed to look like a reporter who was exhausted and filthy in the streets of a war torn city.

The first scene I shot was a little shaky. But I received positive feedback from my director, and we shot the scene again. It seemed to go well after the second take. We shot a third take, just for safekeeping, and then moved on to the next scene. With every positive reaction the director gave me, my confidence was lifted. It was a reminder to me that when you give people positive feedback rather than tear them down, you get positive results. It was one of the greatest professional moments of my life. I became reacquainted with my confidence on the set of a multi-million-dollar movie. When *The Avengers* was released in theaters, it was an event for me and my family. My paragraph of lines was whittled down to a nanosecond. But I was there! I was in the movie! On a hot day in May, on the streets of Cleveland, Ohio, I took control of my fears. I was living my playlist. I put in the work. I played the lead actor in my life. And I felt brilliant!

When my mom sent me a text message to be the lead actress in my life, I knew that she wanted me to set aside my doubts. She wanted me to hold my head up high with confidence. And she wanted me to own my moment. I had to believe in the words "I can do this" when I spoke to myself. You may face opportunities that challenge you in your lifetime. You may feel you're out of your element when those opportunities present themselves. But don't ever say "I can't do this" when it's something you truly desire.

We all need to take advantage of our moment to shine. And you must shine with confidence in your spirit. You must own your moment. You worked for that moment. To be the lead actor in your life, you need to know your story line. Know your best angles. Know where you need to stand and when it's time to sit. Know when it's time to wrap up. And know when it's time to get started. Work for your opportunities. Be prepared for your opportunities. Take advantage of your opportunities. And allow yourself to shine. Be the lead actor in your life.

nine

Going Home Again

Playlist Song & Artist: "The House That Built Me" Miranda Lambert

I was raised in a Catholic family. We went to church every Sunday. I went to an all-girls Catholic high school called Magnificat High School. And from time to time my parents would invite our church pastor over for dinner. I grew up in a beautiful home. It was a redbrick Georgian colonial that sat on two acres near the cul-de-sac at the end of the street. My mom made sure that the house was always landscaped with colorful flowers during the summer, and my dad grew small gardens of tomatoes, zucchini, eggplant, figs, and fresh herbs. In the wintertime, the snow fell perfectly on the hundreds of trees that surrounded our home. And deer pranced around the property looking for food while the *Kenny Rogers Christmas* album played in the background. The house often smelled of my mom's homemade chocolate chip cookies in the oven or a pot of Italian spaghetti sauce bubbling on the stove. There were plenty of kids my age in the neighborhood to play with, and my cousins lived one street away. I would often ride my blue ten-speed bike over to my cousins Jenn and Stephanie's house. From there we would bike together to the local convenience store to buy candy and snacks. Cherry-flavored Tangy Taffy and Rolos were my favorite treats! And once we were teenagers, our parents would allow us to ride our bikes to the neighborhood eatery Sorrento's for lunch. Of all the Sicilian-style menu options that we could sink our teeth into, we often chose the taco pizza for our meal. It was an Italian restaurant, but I remember loving the taco pizza! We had a ravine behind our house that backed up to a river. My brother and I would shimmy down a rope that hung on a tree along a cliff, which took us down to the riverbank. Together, with our backpacks filled with Coke bottles and oranges, we spent hours hanging out by the water and exploring nature.

My parents belonged to a country club. My siblings and I swam at the club pool all day. We sipped on our favorite Slush Puppie flavors and ate microwaved pizza off Styrofoam plates while our parents golfed. As kids, we thought everything at the concession stand was free because we didn't need cash to make a purchase. We only needed to know our ID number. Almost twenty years after my last visit to the concession stand, I still remember that number. We also participated in the club's swim team, which created an opportunity for us to make lifelong friends and develop our first teenage crushes. My crush was on the Castro twins. They had dark hair, brown eyes, tanned skin, and perfect smiles. Since there were two of them and they were identical, I usually liked the one who was single and would give me the time of day. Which was almost never. Maybe because I was a skinny kid with clear braces. But even during an awkward phase, a girl can dream.

My siblings and I had a happy childhood. We weren't perfect kids, but my parents would probably say that we were close to perfect. We didn't do drugs. We all had nice friends. And we rarely got into trouble. Okay, maybe I got into trouble for mouthing off during my bratty teenage years, but that's a rite of passage for a young girl. The town I grew up in and my old neighborhood were symbolic of very happy times for me. It was a time of structure, responsibility, and discipline. But it was also a time when my only worry was getting home before the streetlights came on at night. I reached a point in my life where I longed to reconnect with that part of my past. A past that was pure, simple, and carefree.

Many years after I moved away from home, I found myself in a position where my life seemed out of focus. I lost my job after spending many years building my career. I was well into my thirties and single again with a desire to have a home and my own family. Have you ever felt you've reached a point where you had to start your life over again? That's how I felt, but I didn't know where to start. My life seemed stagnant. And my future felt uncertain. In the movie *Up in the Air,* George Clooney's character asks the question, "How much does your life weigh?" My life felt as if it weighed nothing because I had nothing of my own. Yet I felt the weight of the world on my shoulders because I had a questionable future that I wanted to define for myself. But when I looked into my future, I felt lost. This feeling of limbo led me to a place that was always steady in my life. I needed to get back to my roots. I wanted to fix what was broken inside of me. So I went home to the house that built me.

Going home allowed me to quietly assemble an army of protection around me while I figured out the direction of my life. It was a place where I felt safe from bad people and poor decision making. At home, no one cared if I had interviewed George Clooney or Matt Damon the day before. And they didn't judge me for going through setbacks. My family wanted to see me survive my fall and succeed again. The house that built me wasn't about the beautiful brick structure or the detailed interior design. It was about the people who loved and supported me. These people helped me to shape my core values.

Financially it made sense to move home. I didn't have a job, so it was foolish to spend money on rent. Plus, my money was quickly running out. But still it was hard to shake the idea that I was a thirty-six-year-old woman living at home with my parents. How embarrassing! I continued to tell friends that I was living in my old apartment. In fact, I was picked up and dropped off at my old apartment many times when I was no longer at that address. This became challenging when I went on dates. But I figured out a way to make it work and kept the location of where I slept at night private. I would wave good-bye at the end of the night and find a sneaky way of walking to my car. And then I would drive off to my real home. Those who did know where I was living didn't judge me. My closest friends and family felt it was the best place for me to be at the time. I was focused on becoming stronger. The home I grew up in helped me build my strength.

I started going to church again with my parents on Sundays. It was the church I attended as a child and a place where I felt comfortable. I took walks and jogs every morning on the street where I used to play as a kid. The sights, the sounds, the neighbors, they were all familiar to me. And with every lap I took around the block, my neighbors' waves and smiling faces felt like cheers of support as I was running my personal marathon of life. I slept in the room that I called my own as a young girl. The wallpaper and paint were different from the bright peach room where I spent twenty years dreaming. The walls were updated to a shade of cream, bordered by subtle pink and green flowers. The new carpeting was plush and a soft ivory tone. But the cherrywood furniture was still the same from years ago. On top of my dresser sat an old framed article from the local paper, the *Chronicle Telegram*. The article was titled "Elyria Native Lands Local Talk Show Gig." It was printed on Sunday, August 28, 2005, and included my picture on the front page of the paper. It was an accessory my mom added to my bedroom to display her pride in me. The view from my bedroom windows was pictur-esque. The summer I moved home, I woke up every morning to a beautiful view of green trees that led to the ravine that my brother and I used to explore as kids. And the birds were always chirping their daily song, which I heard through the windows that were cracked open. My bathroom was a sanctuary. The colors were warm, the lighting could be dimmed, and the skylight over the bathtub gave the room a sense of serenity from the sky above. I took baths every night in the Jacuzzi tub my mom installed to replace the old one. I was safe. I was comfortable. I was loved. I was finding peace and becoming reacquainted with myself. Every day. A little bit at a time.

Reconnecting with my past was an important part of my healing process. I spent time with childhood friends, and we reminisced about old times. The memories from years ago made me happy. I spent more quality time with my parents. My mom and I would make sun tea, sit on the back patio in our bare feet, and have thoughtful and happy conversations. And when my dad came home from work, I would join him outside for a talk while he smoked his favorite cigar. I often went to the market and prepared homemade dinners for my parents, using many of the techniques I learned on my old television show from talented chefs. I also tried many Barefoot Contessa recipes, such as her lobster rolls and lemon cake with homemade lemon curd. I drove my niece Anna to kindergarten a few times a week. She didn't say much in the car, but it still felt like a bonding moment between me and my six-year-old niece. Whenever I got sad, I tried to spend time with my nieces and nephews. They were all under the age of six, and they made me happy. Their love for me was pure. They didn't want anything from me except my love and attention. And maybe some sugary treats, which were gladly handed out in the form of PEZ, gummy bears, and trips to Menchie's Frozen Yogurt.

During this time, I also stopped drinking alcohol. Not because I had a drinking problem. But sometimes too many drinks can lead a person to do something that they may later regret. You know the times when you've had a few too many cocktails and "liquid courage" kicks in? That liquid courage usually causes you to make a phone call or send a text message that you regret the next morning. I did not want to reach out to any of the bad people who were once in my life. And I certainly didn't want to do it under the influence of alcohol. I wanted to make all of my decisions with a clear head. After many months of healing, when I was feeling stronger, I enjoyed good wine and Tito's vodka again.

I was extremely choosy about who I spent my time with, and I started to notice that I felt better around positive people. When you spend your time with like-minded, goal-oriented, and positive people, it makes you feel good. I had many friends who were athletes. Some at a professional level and others who played in college. I noticed something about my athlete friends. They were all highly motivated and spiritual people. They challenged me physically and mentally when I spent time with them. These were people who had to work hard and overcome obstacles to reach their goals. I had something to learn from these friends. And I'm so grateful they were in my life during this part of my journey.

I've already mentioned that one of my dearest friends in life is Olympic gold medalist Dominique Moceanu. Dominique was a member of the 1996 US Women's Olympic Gymnastics team. She wrote a wonderful book called *Off Balance* about her life as a young gymnast, the challenges she faced throughout her life, and how she overcame major obstacles to reach her goals. Dominique also writes very poignant stories about family, heartbreak, and the public highs and lows of her life. Not only is Dominique a lovely person with a kind heart, she is a woman who gained strength while facing life's challenges. Dominique's challenges gave her more depth, which provided her with great insight as she often counseled me through my personal hurdles.

One night I was out to dinner with Dominique and her husband, Mike. We were dining on delicious steaks and a bottle of Cabernet. The evening was filled with great storytelling, including our adventures from traveling the world and thoughts on where our future travels might take us. I felt comfortable talking to this couple about my current state of limbo. They were both astute listeners. And very perceptive people. When I finished speaking, their words had great impact on me. Dominique and Mike rallied me with their motivational ideas about doing important things with my life and aiming for loftier goals. My friends believed that I had a greater purpose in life. They assured me that I would find my way and that I needed to define my new goals. Their words were empowering. And that night's theme of empowerment carried over into the next week when Dominique and I decided to take a self-defense class together. That class represented a turning point for me in my life.

I'm five feet eight and Dominique stands at five feet four. We decided to go to a private self-defense class together. The Olympic gold medalist and me. My only award for athleticism was the MVP trophy I won from the Elyria Country Club swim team when I was sixteen years old. And it was probably a sympathy award because it was my last year of eligibility on the team. Dominique and I walked into the self-defense class...a world-class athlete and a country club MVP swimmer. Standing together, we were somewhat of an oxymoron. One of the best athletes in the world was next to someone who, to be honest, wasn't even good at kickball! It turned out that none of that mattered. Dominique and I had the best time! And the great part about going to this class with Dominique was that she pushed herself to perfect the self-defense moves we were taught and wanted to learn more complicated skills. When I watched her do this, it motivated me to want to do more. If I had gone to the class alone that day, I would have stayed for an hour and tried not to make a fool of myself. But with my friend by my side, I stayed an extra hour and pushed myself to work harder. Dominique got me to go outside of my own physical and mental boundaries. She was representative of the kind of friend I wanted in my life. Dominique was a woman who challenged me to be a better person. Always try to surround yourself with someone who inspires you to be a better version of yourself. People who bring that gift to you will enhance your life in ways that are life changing.

When I went home from my self-defense class that day, my parents saw a change in my spirit. Their daughter was coming back to life. I had been struggling all summer long. After months of crying and bouts of self-diagnosed depression, a spark ignited within me. I had a little extra pep in my step. I was smiling and laughing as I told my parents about my day. And I even tried to teach them a few of the self-defense moves that I learned. Physically challenging myself was a confidence booster. I needed to continue challenging myself. When we push ourselves, we always move forward. And after life's setbacks, you want to make choices that move you toward progression.

I had a couple of friends who hosted radio shows in town. From time to time these friends would call me to fill in as a cohost. These were extremely important moments for boosting my confidence level. By using my ad lib skills in a broadcast environment, I felt a sense of self-worth. I came alive in the studio! These opportunities gave me a chance to perform on the air, usually off the cuff, and I loved that challenge! It was great to be a part of a team, even if it was just from time to time. This work allowed me to keep my skills fresh. And even though they were just fill-in gigs, my parents were proud of my talents and encouraged me to continue looking for work in my field of expertise. While I was the host of my own television show for years, some people wondered if my pride got in the way by doing fill-in jobs on the radio. It was the exact opposite. Pride was no longer an issue for me. When you take a big fall, you can't let your ego get in the way of the climb back up. But you can't lose sight of your own strengths and skills either. When I sat in on the radio shows, I put my strengths and skills to work. And honestly, some of my favorite professional moments happened while I was talking behind the radio microphone. I felt no pressure because the radio shows weren't riding on my shoulders. I could be my authentic self on the radio. And I didn't have to edit my own thoughts or worry if I was going to offend anyone. It was a time of pure fun. And I needed to find the fun in broadcasting again. I wasn't sure if I was going back into that business full time, but my guest hosting opportunities reminded me that I still had talent.

Going home again was a humbling experience. I learned that being humbled is a good thing. It makes you appreciate where you came from. It helps you refocus on what you're working toward. And it makes you accept everything that happens in between that time. Being humbled reminds you that anyone can have setbacks. But in order to get out of your slump, it's important to align yourself with people who empower and encourage you when you fall back. Going home again helped me take leaps forward after I fell backward. It was important for me to reconnect with my roots because that is where the foundation of my character was first formed. When you're struggling, find the people and places that give you strength and remind you of your foundation. And as you're living your playlist, reflect on the pieces and parts of the house that built you. We all need to remember our foundation from time to time. Wherever or whatever that may be.

ten

Eminem Said Not to Quit

Playlist Song & Artist: "'Till I Collapse" Eminem

Do you ever feel defeated? Beaten down? Depressed? As if you're a breath away from giving up? I did. And I needed a large dose of motivation to keep going. To push forward. To run away from what knocked me down. And run toward success. I found that extra push of adrenaline in a rapper from Detroit. The rapper's music was feeding my motivation every time I popped in my earphones and pushed "play" on my playlist. My workouts were key to my healing process. And I needed the right music to feed my soul during my workouts. When you work out, your body releases endorphins. Endorphins are natural pain and stress fighters. And I needed a lot of endorphins! Trust me, I know that when you get depressed, the last thing you want to do is go for a walk, a run, a bike ride, or anything that requires physical activity. But you need to motivate yourself to move! It will make you feel better. Even if it's just temporary relief. And sometimes that's all we need. A temporary fix to get us through a difficult moment.

Personally, my workouts helped me make healthy decisions. Without them, I would have fallen into a deep depression after

I lost my job and pieces of myself in an unhealthy relationship. I treated my daily workouts as something I had to do in order to survive. And I discovered an unlikely friend during my workouts. Rapper Eminem. No, I don't know him personally. But his music spoke to me. He wrote about pain that I could feel. He rapped about life moments that I experienced. His words spoke about some of the same anger that I felt. Eminem's lyrics motivated me. And the rhythm of his music kept me on beat to keep moving and work through my pain.

The first time I started working out to Eminem's music was during my cycling classes. I found a place that I loved to work out at called Psycle. And Psycle wasn't just a workout, it was mental and physical therapy! It was like church for the body and soul. My instructor, Jenn, who eventually became one of my most cherished friends, was kick ass in every way! Jenn stood at six feet tall with a body like Sigourney Weaver's, but with bigger boobs. Her dark hair was chin length and always pulled back in a bandana. Her voice was powerful, but not the least bit annoying. Jenn got up on her bike, in front of a sold-out class, and motivated us as if we were riding to the Promised Land. The room was dark with a few dim lights and candles burning an aromatherapy scent of eucalyptus. Jenn talked about coming to class with an intention for our lives. And she encouraged us to push ourselves to our limit. And then push a little harder. Jenn reminded us that our bodies were amazing tools, capable of doing things we didn't think were possible if we could be open to change. And she talked about making positive changes every day, no matter how big or small. Jenn told us that sweat cleanses the parts of our bodies that a shower can't reach. As a studio full of riders pedaled to the beat of the music, with drenched bodies and a burning fire in our legs, Jenn would yell out, "I didn't say it would be easy, I said it would be worth it!" She was right, the ride wasn't easy. I was physically exhausted. And at that time in my life, I was mentally drained. But with each pedal stroke and drip of sweat, I became stronger. And I started cleaning out all of the negativity in my heart and mind. When I first discovered Jenn's cycling classes, my professional life felt uncertain. I had a career, but I wasn't happy where I was working anymore. And I believed that my talents were not being fully utilized. I also had a lot of toxic people in my life at this time. I desired something more for myself. A more fulfilled life. A happier and healthier life. And I knew I could get there if I worked through my insecurities, self-doubt, and the limitations that I felt had been placed upon me. And truth be told, I was placing limitations on myself. It's important to recognize when you place limitations on yourself. If you don't recognize this and proactively release the chains that bind you, then you will stay in a stagnant rut. I knew I had to work hard to reach my goals. I needed to push my body and challenge my mind. I believed that the work I put into myself would see positive results. In all aspects of my life. We cannot allow our weaknesses or fear to guide our decision making. That exact message came through every time Jenn played Eminem's music during her class. This is when I realized that I needed to put his music on my playlist.

I remember the first time I bought an Eminem CD. It was years before I started working out regularly. I was in my midtwenties. I bought one of his albums because I liked a song on the radio called "The Way I Am." But when I listened to the entire CD, the music sounded angry. And it kind of scared me. I did not have the same feelings that Eminem was rapping about. I couldn't relate to his words. He seemed so pissed in every song. But after going through some painful experiences in my life, his music started speaking to me. I connected with the pain he wrote about. Once you feel true pain, it creates an understanding between you and others who have also been scarred by pain. And it gives you more depth of understanding when you hear their stories. Songs like "Lose Yourself," "Love the Way You

Lie," "Cinderella Man," and "Till I Collapse" fueled my energy to work through my pain. And I became motivated to succeed. I told myself that I would rise to professional success again. And I made a promise to myself that there would be no room for toxic relationships in my life. I might have fallen down, but it was time to get back up. Eminem's music was vital to me while I was living my playlist.

When I started to look for work again, I faced rejection after rejection. Some businesses never called me back. And the local television stations in my town told me that they didn't have any opportunities for me. I couldn't get an agent to sign me. And my contacts who said they would help me never came through. A few months after I lost my job, it was announced that the show I formerly hosted was being cancelled and replaced by a new show. At the time of that announcement, I received a personal e-mail from my former boss explaining some of the details of this new show. It was a painful e-mail to receive. I had been let go. And then replaced. Months passed. And now I was reading about my replacement in a personal e-mail? Was this really happening? If an NFL quarterback lost his starting position and was let go from the team, would the coach contact him after his release and tell him about his replacement? I think it's safe to assume that scenario would not happen. The e-mail I received made me feel horrible. And my confidence was deeply shaken. I was doubting myself. And with my doubt came internal questions. Maybe I wasn't good at what I did. Maybe I didn't have talent. Why didn't anyone want to hire me? Wasn't I good enough to be hired? These were all thoughts that went through my mind. But every time I started to get down on myself, I listened to Eminem and went for a workout.

When my confidence was shot, I also turned to people who cared about me for affirmation. I was honest about my self-doubt with them. I told them that I was questioning my own level of talent. I expressed worry that no one was ever going to hire me. My family and friends gave me positive affirmation. And that is vital. When you lose confidence in yourself, sometimes you need to rely on people you trust to keep you from shutting down. My family, friends, and a couple of close colleagues reminded me that I was talented and that I had many good qualities to offer an employer. This positive affirmation didn't get me a job, but it did keep me motivated to not give up.

This was also a time when I needed to take a look at myself and my mistakes. Taking an honest look at yourself and knowing what you've done wrong in life is a necessary part of the journey. It ultimately makes you a better person. I believe in focusing on people's strengths and not their weaknesses. I think that you get the best out of someone when you develop their strengths rather than point out their shortcomings. But when you're analyzing yourself, you must come face to face with your own mistakes. You must learn from them and stop making them. It's the only way to move toward a wiser and better you. Once I was able admit my professional mistakes and correct them, I knew I would be a better employee and a better person.

MISTAKE #1: When I didn't get the raises I thought I deserved, I became less dedicated to my job. This is a mistake, because I think you should always give 100 percent to any job or task. You don't ever want to do something half-assed, especially when it has your name written all over it. When my employer didn't give me a raise, I interpreted that as meaning my employer didn't value my work. What I should have done was look for a job with a pay increase, if money was that important. Or at the very least, find another employer who promised the ability to raise my salary over time. I think it's important to know your value in the workplace. Never devalue yourself. But equally, never devalue your work ethic. Raise or no raise. Your name and your work are representative of your character. Be a person of good character.

MISTAKE #2: I got caught up in office gossip. This is so bad and so easy to do. One day you're minding your own business and trying to block out the gossipy chatter going on around you. And the next thing you know, you're participating in the chatter. Talking poorly about other people is mean. Talking about other people is the behavior of playground bullies. It's always best to look people in the eye and tell them your concerns. You'll get more respect out of them when you do. And you'll feel better about being up front with them rather than talking behind their backs. When you gossip, you're being unkind. When you're up front, you're the kind of person people will respect and trust.

MISTAKE #3: I let the inmates run the asylum. At one point in my career, I was managing a team of people. While my personality is extremely alpha, I don't enjoy confrontation. In a work environment, not all personalities are going to mix well. My strength is that I'm a good listener when there are problems. My weakness was that I allowed the problems to get out of hand. When there was conflict, I tried to be a people pleaser and make sure that everyone was happy. But when the conflict had a clear-cut resolution, I should have been more firm about that resolution. There were times when I encountered work situations that got out of control. And even the people who looked to me as their superior had to wonder whether or not I was in charge. I was letting the inmates run the asylum. That was a big mistake. If you're in charge, it's important to maintain control over situations involving conflict.

MISTAKE #4: I started to feel entitled. I felt entitled to more money. I felt entitled to the perks that came with the position. And I felt a great sense of self-importance. After I lost my job, my father reminded me that it's good to be humbled every now and then. I learned the importance of humility the hard way. But it was good for me. The first job that I had after my months of unemployment was a production job. One day while

I was at work, the company needed someone to create goodie baskets for a few important clients. I was assigned the job. Some people might snicker at this and say, wow, a year ago she was interviewing the cast of the *Twilight* movies and now she's making goodie baskets? But I actually loved it! It was therapeutic, and I was determined to create the kind of baskets that would make Martha Stewart proud! Plus, it didn't hurt that I was being paid well to perform this simple task. My rise and fall in the land of opportunity made me appreciate having a job, whatever that job might be. It made me appreciate the value of working hard and earning a dollar. And in a tough economy, it made me realize that a job is a gift. We are never too good for the work that we do. But we should strive to be excellent in every job that we have.

A change was happening. I was a work in progress. As I was working on myself, I chose to seek the wisdom of people who seemed at peace in life. I looked to people who were once knocked down but who beat their own challenges. These people weren't trying to keep up with their neighbors or fit in with the cool crowd. And they didn't get caught up in gossip or speak negatively about others. These were people who found happiness. And I wanted to know how to be a truly happy person. One of my great teachers in achieving happiness is my personal trainer, Mike.

Back when I was still working in television, I flew to Philadelphia to interview Tom Hanks for one of his upcoming films. It was the second time I interviewed Tom during my career. It should be noted that this was not the time I was overcome by full-body perspiration while interviewing Mr. Hanks. I was taking a day trip from Cleveland to Philadelphia for the interview, but I had many hours of down time between the interview and my departure flight. The movie studio gave me a hotel room in which to relax for the day so that I wasn't homeless in Philadelphia. While I was staring out of my hotel room and looking at the historic and busy streets below, I contemplated where to go for my first authentic Philly cheesesteak. Somewhere between thoughts of provolone cheese and Cheez Whiz, I noticed my reflection in the window. I was looking more swollen in shape than my usual self. Could it be from air travel? My flight to Philly had been less than two hours. I couldn't be that swollen from travel. I put my hands around my waist. I was feeling thicker than I remembered my once slim self. I didn't like how I felt, and suddenly my mood was as gloomy as the overcast skies. I had a small epiphany in that moment. It was time to get my body in shape again! I picked up my cell phone and called Mike, my former trainer. A few years prior, Mike helped me reach my fitness goals. But between my busy schedule and stresses in my work and personal life, I stopped taking care of myself. I told Mike I wanted to recommit myself to a healthy lifestyle. He sounded pleased to get my call and was excited to work with me again. Mike was instrumental during my journey to adopt a healthy mind, body, and soul. From the moment I made that phone call in my hotel room, I was committed to my weekly workouts. Mike's philosophy was simple: 1. Work out most days of the week. 2. Eat well and watch your portions. 3. Be sure to get a good night's sleep. 4. Keep your stress level low.

I knew that Mike practiced the philosophy that he taught, but there was something special about his aura. He always seemed at peace and genuinely happy. Mike came from humble and difficult beginnings. As a young boy, Mike was poor and didn't receive much attention at home from his family. At one point in his young life, Mike told me that he started running around with the wrong crowd. Today Mike admits that many of his childhood friends ended up in prison. But as a young man, Mike made a conscious decision to make a good life for himself. He committed to practicing an all-encompassing healthy lifestyle. Mike told me about a happiness course he took online through Harvard. It's one of the most popular courses taken through the university. Mike told me that one of the homework assignments was to write down three things every day that made you happy. It was a daily assignment that caused people to reflect on three positive things that happened throughout their day. I have no scientific evidence to say how this task affected the students taking the class. But I do know that my trainer, Mike, who practices this task, is one of the kindest and happiest people that I know. And through his happiness, he appears to be at peace.

I decided to adopt this practice of happiness and gratitude. Every night when I rest my head on my pillow, I reflect on three things that deserve my gratitude. It might be something big, like getting a promotion. But typically it's something more basic and meaningful, like taking a long walk in the park with someone special or receiving a surprise phone call from an old friend. Mike's workouts inspired me to be physically fit. But it's his practice of gratitude that inspires me to be mentally fit. Mike is a successful businessman, but it's his positive energy that stands out the most when I'm around him. If you make just one change in your life today, make it the practice of gratitude.

Positive energy is infectious, especially when you allow your soul to let it in. My soul felt good any time I visited an older couple I knew on the other side of town, Jan and Sheldon. Jan is a former television talk show host. Sheldon is a retired plastic surgeon. They both had previous marriages that failed, but when they met, they fell in love. Their love is palpable when they are together in a room. Later in life, Sheldon, or Shelly, as his wife calls him, suffered a heart attack. He had a heart transplant. But his body rejected his new heart. Shelly was extremely ill, and the next twenty-four hours were touch and go. Shelly received a second heart, and his body embraced the new life that it gave him. I remember when Shelly was sick. He was frail and gaunt and his face was ashen. When someone we love is battling for his or her life, we pray, we hope, and sometimes we prepare for the worst. But Jan's faith was unshakable. And her spirit seemed to be unwavering. No doubt she had her quiet, painful moments. But she was a pillar of strength while her husband lay weak in a hospital bed. Today, while many years separate us in age, Jan and Shelly rival most young adults with their youthful spirit.

I went to visit Jan and Shelly one afternoon about a year after I lost my job. They live on a private lot of land surrounded by hundreds of tall trees and not far from a waterfall that is central to the quaint town where they reside. My visit felt like an old-fashioned summer day as I pulled up the long driveway to be greeted by this lovely couple sitting together on their front porch swing. Jan prepared some chilled iced teas. It was a special concoction she spiked with vodka and served with decorated cutout cookies shaped like ladybugs. As we visited on their white front porch in the summer heat, a heavy rainfall swept through town to cool off some of the outdoor humidity. But we hardly seemed to notice the raindrops or change in temperature. We were laughing, sharing stories, and enjoying the afternoon in good spirits. Jan and Shelly lit up every time they looked at each other. And when Jan would excuse herself to refill our drinks, she would give her husband a gentle love tap as she walked past him. Shelly would reciprocate the affection by laying his hand upon hers, even if it was brief. This was a couple who stared death in the face. I can't think of a greater challenge. Today they live life to the fullest by traveling the world, enjoying time with their family, and spending peaceful moments together. I felt grateful to share a moment with them. On their front porch. Watching two lovers who were best friends enjoy the simple pleasures in life.

As I continued to reflect on happy people in my life, I thought about my friend Taylor. I met her through years of covering movie junkets. She also traveled the world interviewing every famous star on the planet. Eventually, like me, she lost her job. And through her writing, Taylor acknowledges one of her greatest losses...suffering a miscarriage. Taylor decided to do her own kind of experiment after living through personal and professional sadness. She called her experiment "The Happygirl Experiment." It's a website/blog that she wrote as a guide to getting your happy back. Her website offers everything from motivational quotes, to recipes that include "fortune cookie chicken" and "hotel-style lemon cheese pancakes," to tips on how to pull off the perfect Walt Disney World proposal. Every morsel of information that my friend wrote about and posted was positive and happy. I felt happy (and hungry) just looking at her website! Taylor's experiment was about focusing on the positives in life. So whether you're happy that you got to walk on the beach and feel the sand between your toes...or indulge in a gooey chocolate brownie...or spend an afternoon sipping iced teas with a good friend, Taylor's point was to enjoy positive and pleasurable moments in life. I could see by the smile in her photographs that Taylor was a happier person. And I knew that she was a woman with a kind and generous spirit. Taylor's journey took her back to her high school in Massachusetts, where she became the director of advancement and alumni relations. It wasn't the glamorous job she once held in the film and entertainment world, but she told me that it gave her great pleasure to improve the educational lives of the students who now attended her beloved alma mater. Simple pleasures were a part of Taylor's healing process. And her choices motivated her to find happiness and fulfillment in her life again.

Eminem's lyrics motivated me while I was living my playlist. And the examples of how happy people lived their lives showed me why I needed to stay motivated. I knew if I stayed committed to motivation and happiness, the payoff would be substantial. Happy people have inner strength. Happy people are not quitters. Happy people strive for goodness. Happy people are infectious, and they want good things for others. Happy people are at peace. Find what it is in life that makes you happy. And use that to fuel your motivation to never give up. Even when life gets tough. Look at yourself in the mirror and tell that person that you will not give up. You will not be a quitter. You will survive your setbacks. You will push yourself through hard times. You will find happiness. And you will succeed. Push "play" and get going!

eleven

Some Things Aren't Worth Fighting For

Playlist Song & Artist: "Live To Tell" Madonna

I grew up loving Madonna and her music. I remember a time when I wished that I looked like her. That was never going to happen, so I settled for dressing up as Madonna on Halloween. As a young girl, it wasn't very appropriate for me to be wearing a black fishnet top, short miniskirt, and red lipstick. And I'm quite certain that I argued the details of the costume with my mother. But because my grandmother sewed the outfit together, my mom let it slide as long as I wore a jean jacket to cover the see-through parts of the shirt. My mom knew I was a good kid who wasn't trying to be provocative. I'm pretty sure my mom decided that my childhood Madonna costume was not something worth fighting over. She knew I was just a kid playing dress-up on a night when a bag full of Kit Kats and Skittles would be consumed in abundance.

Madonna eventually grew out of her punk rock fashion phase and opted for a more polished look. This was around the time that she released the song "Live to Tell." I didn't know then how much the lyrics would impact me today. When I came up with the idea for *Live Your Playlist*, "Live to Tell" was one of the songs that I played often during my thought-filled walks. The song was haunting to me. I connected with it. And it made me reflect on the idea that through heartbreak, we learn powerful lessons about ourselves and others. Over time our lives become an intricate story. And we live to tell lessons that should be passed on to others. One of the things I live to tell is that some things aren't worth fighting for.

For a long time I struggled with the idea that if I didn't fight for something, it meant I was giving up. And I often equated giving up with the negative connotation of quitting. As I searched my memory bank, I tried to discover where that equation came from. My regression took me to my childhood. A time when many of us learn the concept that only quitters give up. Like many children, I was taught not to be a quitter by my parents. And so I fought to the bitter end on everything, even when I wanted to give up. An early example of this happened when I was on a swim team. The hardest part of swim practices for me were the runback sprints. All of the swimmers had to sprint swim from one side of the pool to the other, hop out of the pool, and then run back to our starting positions. Each runback sprint had to happen within sixty seconds. The faster we swam and ran, the more seconds we had to catch our breath before we started our next runback sprint. We did this over and over. It felt like physical torture. And I lost count of how many times I was gasping for air during my runbacks to the starting block. I was winded and in pain. I wanted to quit. But I remember my father yelling out with a smile on his face, "No pain, no gain, Andrea!" And so I kept on sprinting and running until the very end. I couldn't be a quitter. My parents wouldn't allow it.

An example of not quitting in my later years happened after I lost my job. I was on the hunt for a new job and seemed to keep hitting a dead end. I couldn't find work. I was losing confidence in myself and wanted to give up. One day when I told my mom how I felt, she looked at me and said, "You owe it to the girls who look up to you to succeed." My mother's thought was a lovely one, but it made me feel a lot of pressure. Pressure to not let others down. Pressure to be successful. Pressure to live up to my mother's words. And the pressure was getting to me. But the message was clear. I couldn't give up.

The swim team and work stories are two good examples of times when a person should not quit. I wasn't going to die during my runback sprints. I was a healthy young person challenging my body. I was fighting to be a better swimmer and to win races. And when I lost my job, I couldn't give up the search for a new job. I could not quit on myself. I had to fight to succeed in my professional life. So under what circumstances should you quit? How do you decide when something isn't worth fighting for? Maybe you've thought to yourself, "If I quit or give up, it means that I'll lose and someone else wins." Or maybe you view quitting as failing. And no one wants to fail. My response to those thoughts is that it's all about perspective. Sometimes you have to look at a situation through a different lens. I want to share some stories that my friends gave me permission to use. These are stories and examples of when it's time to close the book and walk away from something that is no longer worth fighting for.

An Unhealthy Relationship is not worth fighting for. My girlfriend was married to a guy who was once the man of her dreams. They seemed perfectly matched when they first met. They both came from strong ethnic families. And they lived the motto "work hard, play hard." Eventually they had a couple of beautiful children and moved into a big house in the suburbs. My friend was a stay-at-home mom, and her husband ran the family business. They were living the American Dream and wanted for nothing, from the Range Rover to the Louis Vuitton purses. And then the economy tanked. My friend was selling off her expensive bags to pay for her children's medical bills.

And the high-end car was replaced with a leased car in a more reasonable price range. It was during this time that my friend's husband seemed to lose himself. He came home drunk on a regular basis. And on several occasions he crashed the car into the garage door. Some nights he didn't even come home. My friend would sit up and worry through the early hours of the morning. Her worry eventually turned into rage. And verbal fights at home became a common occurrence.

One morning I met my friend for coffee. Her beautiful face looked worn and tired. She recounted the events that led to the deterioration of her marriage. It had been failing over many years, she said. But my friend was a fighter. She had been her whole life. And she still had love for her husband. Mentally she was drained. Emotionally she had left him. But should she physically stay in that relationship? That was the question she asked herself almost daily. This was a relationship that had many layers. Some good. Some bad. But the bad parts were making my friend sick. And her unhealthy marriage was not one that she wanted her children exposed to every day. My friend fought to keep her marriage going for many years. But it was time for her to decide whether this was a relationship worth fighting for. She worried about money, about being a single mom, about finding a job again, and about being alone. These were all very real fears for her. But after years of arguments that involved profanity, alcohol, and verbal abuse, my friend decided that it was time to walk away from this relationship. She wanted an opportunity for her children to grow up in a peaceful, loving environment. And she hoped that she would find peace in her life too. It was a painful time in her life. But it was the right decision for her. She wasn't quitting. She simply wanted a better life for herself and her children. Eventually my friend met a good man who loved her unconditionally and treated her with respect. He was a great role model for her kids. And together they made a happy, healthy home for their family.

Leaving an unhealthy relationship is not quitting. Unhealthy relationships are not worth fighting for. Logically we know this to be true. So why do we stay in a relationship that causes us stress, anxiety, and tears? Why do we fight to keep something bad alive? If we taste something we don't like, we spit it out. And we usually don't try it again. So when we get a taste of a bad relationship, why do we keep trying? Do we think that eventually it might taste better? That like a good wine it will get better as it ages? We know it will not. Ask yourself a simple question when you're in a bad relationship: "Why am I staying in this relationship?" If you ask yourself why and give an honest answer, you will most likely realize that it's not a good enough reason to stay.

A Toxic Work Environment is not worth fighting for. I got a call from a friend of mine in broadcasting one day. She wanted my opinion on a new job she was auditioning for as cohost of a morning television show. My friend was considered talented by all of her peers. And while she spent years perfecting her craft, she inherently had the "It Factor" that people talk about. The job she was auditioning for was a position that many people in town wanted, but I knew that because of my friend's talents and marketability, she would be a frontrunner to land the job. While everything about the job seemed like a perfect fit for my friend, there was something troubling her. The male host of the show had a reputation for not getting along with any of his female cohosts. In fact, the last handful of female cohosts who worked with this man ended up quitting the show. My friend told me that she heard him trash talk all of those women. During the audition process, my friend experienced traces of this man's bad behavior. He often yelled at the show's staff and belittled them in front of others. While he seemed unprepared, he chose to place the blame on his producers and cohosts for not doing their jobs properly. And his moody behavior bordered on being aggressive and unprofessional, she said. But all of the signs pointed toward my friend getting the job.

The executive producer of the show met with my friend and her agent to discuss money and a contract (in broadcasting, nothing is a sure thing until you sign a contract). And even the male host of the show made remarks to my friend about having her join the show. But something about this job made my friend feel uneasy. Something in her gut told her that she was walking into a toxic work environment. Should she fight for this job, even if it meant risking her own well-being?

The new position would have been a promotion for my friend. It offered higher visibility, more money, and a platform to take her career to the next level. But was it worth emotional stress? Would the stress of a volatile coworker eventually wear her down? Is any amount of money worth being verbally attacked at work? Was a high-profile job a fair exchange for the unprofessional behavior of a work bully? This is a personal choice. But my friend decided that she would not be bullied at work. And I agreed with her choice.

It's difficult to work in an environment when you're battling people who are supposed to be on your team. Challenging your coworkers and even questioning your coworkers is not a bad thing. But embarrassing, humiliating, or bullying your coworkers is unacceptable. Unfortunately, toxic work relationships exist. And I do not believe they are worth fighting for. If you find yourself in a toxic work environment, it may be time to look for another job. Choose to work in an environment where you are wanted, appreciated, and can grow professionally.

Anything That Compromises Your Health and Safety is not worth fighting for. One evening I was out for a walk listening to my playlist on my iPhone. I received a text from a friend asking if I was available to talk. I could sense the worry in her words when she wrote that she needed advice and guidance. I immediately called her back and was met on the other line with tears. My friend was five months pregnant. She had met her baby's father two years prior. They became romantically involved, and the pregnancy was unplanned. But as a couple, they were both excited about the news and decided that they would embrace and adore the new life they created. Halfway into my friend's pregnancy, the father turned back to his unhealthy ways. He was an addict who was overcome by his demons. And he was no longer dependable or supportive of my friend and the pregnancy.

Understandably, my friend was facing a roller coaster of emotions...she was scared, angry, hurt, worried, and felt uncertain about her future. Throw hormones into the mix, and her emotions were firing in all directions. After her tears poured out, the volume in her voice rose, and she proceeded to tell me about the high-powered attorney she planned to hire to collect child support from the father. She would demand that he face his responsibilities and do whatever it took to make that happen! That seemed fair. A father should be responsible for his child. But this situation was complicated. And I wanted to offer my friend another perspective.

This is what we knew for a fact. The baby was coming in four months. The father was an addict who participated in risky, dangerous behavior. He decided that he didn't want to be a father. But he would sporadically show up at my friend's house, under the influence, and challenge her on child support. My pregnant friend was stressed. Her stress caused her anxiety. And the child's father made her angry. His behavior was unhealthy and unsafe. Which made this relationship one that compromised my friend's health and safety. This is not a healthy recipe. And every time my friend got angry with this man, she was giving away her power. I wanted to see her take her power back. My suggestion was to forget the attorney. Forget the lawsuits. And forget the child support. She was about to go to war with a man who had no money and no desire to be a father. My friend was about to spend years fighting someone without getting any results. She was going to waste her money on attorney fees. And worse than that, she was going to give all of her power and energy to a man who was never going to offer anything in return. I challenged her to release him from his obligations. I told her that she was a strong and hardworking woman who could do this as a single mom with the help of her friends and family. I wanted her to stop fighting this battle because it was weakening her. She took my advice. And the moment she stopped wanting something from this man was the moment that she set herself free. The angst was gone. The worry disappeared. She got her freedom back. She was in charge of her life and would not be beaten by an unhealthy person. My friend made the right decision for her baby and herself.

As you live your playlist and listen to the music that helps you work through your unhealthy relationships, remember to ask yourself this question: *Why* am I in this relationship? Be honest with your answer. Listen to your answer. And decide if your answer is a good reason to stay. And then decide if that relationship is really worth fighting for. Will that relationship make you a better person? Will it enhance your life? Does it make you happy? Do you find it fulfilling? Does that relationship bring peace to your life? Think about those questions carefully. And then utilize one of your greatest gifts. Your ability to choose.

twelve

The Gift of Pain and Forgiveness

Playlist Song & Artist: "The Heart of the Matter" Don Henley

This chapter almost didn't make it into the book. I wasn't sure that I could write about something that I, like so many others, struggle with throughout life. I'm hardly a master at the art of forgiveness. But I do know that forgiveness is the most important part of healing. Without it, you cannot find true peace in your life. If you're reading this book, you must need to heal in some area of your life. We all do at some time or another. When I decided to write about forgiveness, the song "The Heart of the Matter" immediately popped into my head. I typically listen to India Arie's version of the song from the *Sex and the City* soundtrack. But when I logged onto YouTube and found a video recording of Don Henley singing his song at a Farm Aid concert in 1990, I hit "repeat" and reflected on his lyrics all afternoon. The words are beautiful, painful, honest, and tender. And the song truly gets down to the heart of the matter, which is the gift of forgiveness. And it is a gift. To yourself.

One day I had a chance meeting with a very spiritual man. He wasn't someone I knew well, but the few times I had conversations of depth with him were enlightening moments for me. His schedule was demanding, but he still made time to sit down and talk with me. I didn't mean for it to happen, but because I was struggling with great pain when I met him, it took no more than thirty seconds for every painful emotion I buried deep within to rise to the surface in full force. I was a human volcano, spraying tears, sobs, and gasps of my breath everywhere. I cried about how my heart and soul had been broken. I could hardly bear the pain anymore. And I just wanted to heal. I wanted my sadness to go away. This man looked at me with a peaceful serenity and told me that I must learn to forgive. Not for those who hurt me, but for myself. I asked him if I needed to forgive my offenders in person. He told me no, I just needed to forgive in my heart. And so that journey began. And I'll be honest with you, it's still continuing.

How do you forgive someone who has hurt you to your core? How do you forgive yourself when you've done something that you deem as shameful? How do you release the very thing that you carry around like dead weight day after day? How do you dissolve the feelings of anger that seem to linger when you are reminded of what caused your pain? You begin by acknowledging that you need to forgive. And then you have faith that time will get you to that place of peace. Forgiveness cannot be forced. And it doesn't have a deadline. You can't wish for it to happen overnight. You must give it time. And I believe it helps to pray for the ability to forgive.

Maybe you're like me and you have a hard time forgiving someone because you feel you're letting them off the hook when they don't deserve it. Deep down you want them to suffer for the pain that they've caused you. You may even pull out the bad karma card by telling yourself that what goes around comes around. And you look for solace in that overused phrase. But I challenge you to do something that I've given a lot of thought to...change your perspective. Don't make forgiveness about someone else. Make it about you. Believe in the fact that when you forgive, you're actually helping yourself move forward. You are not setting someone else free from the pains they caused you. You are setting yourself free from the pains that you've carried. When you wish something bad upon someone else, it requires negative thoughts. Those thoughts turn into negative energy and will ultimately rot inside of you. When you allow yourself to be consumed by negative thoughts, you feed your anger. Do not feed anything associated with hate. When you do this, you're placing importance on someone or something that harmed you instead of placing importance on yourself. Make a choice to put yourself first.

I know you're still thinking, "Easier said than done." Right? All of this sounds great. And logically, it makes sense. But we're still human. We hurt when we're broken. We get mad when we're disappointed. And we place blame when we've been wronged. I wrote in an earlier chapter about something I simply refer to as my "five-week fall." To date, it was the worst time in my life. And I was suffering terrible emotional pain. I wanted to medicate myself. I cried every day. And when I wasn't crying, I was angry as hell. I trapped myself in my negative emotions. But I was still able to make an important decision. I decided to feel the pain. I didn't mask it with pills. I let myself cry. And I ran through my anger. But the important part of my decision was allowing myself to *feel* the pain. You can only mask your pain for so long. Eventually you have to face it, feel it, experience it, and, in time, heal from it. Once you heal and release yourself from the pain, you'll reach a place of forgiveness. My five-week free fall actually lasted for a couple of years. But once I learned forgiveness, I landed on solid ground.

Children can teach us important lessons without meaning to. My brother and his wife have four children. They took an out of town trip for a week while the babysitter and I took turns parenting. I was out running errands when I got a panicked call from the babysitter. My one-year-old nephew fell and busted his lip on the floor. I could hear his deafening screams in the background. The sitter was equally upset because the baby had blood on his lip after the fall. Typically calm in a moment of crisis, I told her, "He's crying. Which means he's breathing. And if he's breathing, then he's alive. I'm sure he's going to be fine." It was a minor injury, and my nephew had already moved on to plowing over his older sisters by the time I came home.

My nephew's injury was a physical pain more than an emotional pain. But the lesson in that story can work for all types of pain. If you're feeling pain and breathing through it, then you're alive. Which certainly beats the alternative. Feeling pain is better than not feeling anything at all. Pain tells you that something is wrong and needs to be fixed. Sometimes we tell ourselves that it's better to numb our pain. But when it comes to pains of the heart, I think it's better to feel and fight our way through the hurt. It's the only way to give ourselves a chance to properly heal. Emotional pain is almost always felt when we need to forgive. And if you're open to the journey that pain and forgiveness take you on, you'll find that they become beautiful complements to each other in your life.

There are endless reasons to offer forgiveness. I want to touch on the three that I've found to be the most difficult but ultimately the most loving:

1. Forgive them even if they're not sorry.
2. Forgive to make things right.
3. Forgive yourself. You've already been forgiven.

Forgive them even if they're not sorry. This takes incredible strength of character. It takes a person with a kind and open heart to do this. Sometimes you are never going to get an apology. Many people struggle with the words "I'm sorry." Or they offer a disingenuous apology. And sometimes they refuse to say the words because they don't think that they've done anything wrong. Or maybe they don't care enough about you to apologize. Whatever the reason, you are left hurt and with no sense of remorse from the other person. When this happens, you feel no closure on a painful experience. Sometimes we have to give ourselves closure. And this is why you want to forgive people even if they are not sorry. Through your forgiveness, you close a chapter of your life that is no longer worth revisiting. You will be making peace with a bad experience. And that hurtful experience will no longer occupy space in your mind. You are now releasing that hurt through your forgiveness. And you did it for *you*.

Forgive to make things right. A good friend of mine once told me, "You don't have to be right to get your way." Think about that statement. It's so true. Sometimes we hesitate to forgive out of stubbornness. We want to be right. We believe that we are. And we demand that the other person take the blame for any wrongdoing. If someone you care about hurts you, and this person is worthy of remaining in your life, you must forgive him or her.

Let me share a personal example of how I used the words "I'm sorry" and forgiveness to make things right. I'm blessed to be very close to my family. We are a strong unit. But we definitely have our moments. I love my sister, Kathleen. But when we fight, our alpha personalities collide. And we crashed hard after a heated phone conversation. I was coming off a tough year, having faced many personal challenges. She was the mother of two small children, working a full-time job, with a husband who worked two jobs and went to school part time. As the older sister, I often played the role of my sister's counselor in life. When she struggled, I was there to get her back on track. Now that I was struggling, I needed my sister's counsel. I tried to reach out to my sister for weeks, but she was not returning my phone calls. Eventually this angered me, and I left her a mean voice message to let her know how I felt. She called me back the next day, practically in tears, but she also made some nasty comments that felt dismissive of my personal struggles. We reached a stalemate on the phone. I wasn't budging on my accusation that my sister was not there for me when I needed her most. And my sister called me a bitch for my ruthless tone and not understanding her busy schedule. After she cursed at me, she hung up the phone. That made me even angrier! So I proceeded to text her these words: *Don't. Ever. Speak. To. Me. Again!* The grudge holder in me made up my mind. My sister and I would never speak again! And it would be her loss, I bitterly thought to myself. I was always there for my sister and now when I needed her, she was using a crying baby and work as her excuse? How dare she? That's what I thought when I hung up the phone and divorced her as my sister.

This is an example of two strong personalities who were not willing to look at the situation from someone else's perspective. I thought my sister was dismissive and ignored me when I needed her. And she thought that I was being unreasonable by not understanding that she was overworked, overtired, and her mommy duties were in overdrive. But when I thought about it more clearly, I came to an important conclusion. I loved my sister. And I knew that she loved me. She was my best friend in life. Sure, we had just cursed each other to high heaven. And when I hung up the phone, I thought we'd had the kind of fight to end our relationship. But she was my family. We cared for each other more than we fought. And yes, we said some hurtful words. But they were spoken in a moment of rage and we didn't mean what we said. This kind of fight deserved an apology. After a couple of days, we contacted each other. We both apologized. And we both forgave each other. In the end, forgiveness made things right again.

Forgive yourself. You've already been forgiven. I think this is the hardest form of forgiveness. Forgiving ourselves when we've done something that makes us feel ashamed, embarrassed, or regretful. We are hardest on ourselves. We punish ourselves. And we often can't seem to forgive ourselves when we've done something morally wrong. While I have strong faith, I never intend to push my religious beliefs on anyone with my story-telling. But I want to share a simple story with you that taught me about the reason to forgive yourself. One of the sacraments that Catholics participate in is confession. I remember going to confession in grade school, when the only "sin" I could confess was lying to my parents or being mean to my brother or sister. I was told by the priests to recite the Our Father a few times and all would be forgiven. At least that's how I remember it. As an adult, I rarely went to confession. But the older I got, the more questionable decisions I made. Eventually poor decisions catch up with you and weigh heavily on your mind. And so, as a late-twentysomething-year-old, I went back to confession. I told the priest about something I had done that I deemed "shame-ful." And of course I started crying. Somewhere between the sobs and sniffles, I said that I would never be able to forgive myself. Looking back, my emotions were a bit dramatic. But it was something that bothered me at the time. And it became a life-changing moment for me. I'll never forget the words this priest said to me in that small confession room. He said, "God forgives you. And who are you to think that you are greater than God to not forgive yourself?" And then the room went silent. I don't even remember hearing my own breath. The power of his words hit me like a lightning bolt. I looked at him with watery eyes and could feel the weight of my shame lifted. His question didn't need a verbal response from me. I nodded my head with the realization that he was right. And then I thanked him with my eyes without speaking the words. It was in that moment that I understood why we must forgive our own trespasses.

Forgiveness. It's a beautiful act. But a difficult action. There is no easy way to forgive. But once you digest your hurt, work toward forgiveness. Sometimes you may find yourself ready to forgive, and then suddenly you'll have a setback and change your mind. The road to forgiveness can be a long battle of tug-of-war with your emotions. It takes a lot of strength to forgive. But if you can open your heart to the possibility of forgiveness, you're already heading in a good direction.

thirteen

Don't Be Ruled By "What-Ifs"

Playlist Song & Artist: "Eye of the Tiger" Survivor

I think it's impossible not to be motivated when the *Rocky III* theme song "Eye of The Tiger" starts playing! The hook on the song is so strong. The moment you hear the beat of the music, you're reminded that it's a song about making a comeback and rooting for the underdog. You know this before you even hear the lyrics. No matter how tired my legs were during a workout or how out of breath I felt, when this song kicked in on my playlist, I was fully recommitted to my workout. This song gave me a second wind, and I was always ready to give it 100 percent!

After I lost my job, I couldn't go anywhere without being asked rapid-fire questions: What happened? Why did you leave the show? Did you lose your job? What are you going to do next? When will you be back on TV? Did you leave TV to start a family? Are you getting married? Are you moving to LA for work? How are you making money now? My head was spinning from all of the questions. And quite frankly, the questions gave me anxiety. I felt as if I was trying to make my way through a carnival fun house...trapped, confused, and wondering if I would ever find my way out. Some of these people were curious, some were nosey, and most probably didn't know what to say so they tried to make innocent conversation. But whether we like it or not, when we make a life change, the obvious question that people want to know is what's next? It's a fair question. The problem is that when we don't have an answer, the stress of why-are-you-asking-me-so-many-questions kicks in.

Think of an area in your life that's a sensitive topic. Maybe it's a job loss. Or a divorce. Maybe it's a miscarriage, trouble conceiving, or not wanting to conceive at all. Maybe you have an illness and you just don't care to share all of the details with people. When someone starts asking too many questions about something you don't want to talk about, you either want to smack them in the face or crawl into a hole and never come out. Why? Because their questions are either an invasion of your privacy or you don't have an answer. And if you're like me, you hate it when you don't have an answer. I was raised to believe that "I don't know" is not an answer. Every time someone asked me what I was doing for work after I lost my job, I wanted to either run the other way or hang my head out of embarrassment because I was unemployed. A good friend in the entertainment business told me that I should start telling people that I was shooting adult films. I knew he was trying to be funny. But he also suggested that this answer might put a muzzle on all of the questions I was getting about my next career move. I never shot porn. And I never used that as my answer. Well, maybe I did once just to see the reaction on someone's face. But the smirk on my face couldn't hide the fib I was telling. Joking aside, my search for a respectable answer continued. I considered what my former neighbor used to say when he thought people asked too many questions. In a back-off tone, his response was always, "What? Are you writing a book?" He had the disposition to get away with that kind of response. I knew I would sound like an asshole if I said that to anyone. So I continued to fumble and feel frustrated every time someone asked me a question about my past, present, or future.

One day I had lunch with a life coach (who is someone you should seek out if you feel you're in limbo). A life coach can help you find clarity in your thoughts and outline a plan for your goals. When you feel as if you've lost direction in your life, a life coach can help you get on track and map out your destination. Over a two-hour lunch, my destination was laid out. I had an answer to the questions people were asking. The life coach helped me define what I wanted to do during my post-television stage of life. I decided that I was now a writer. It was time to tell people that I was working on my first book and that this was my full-time job. I now worked for myself. I was going to finish my book and get it to a publisher. When people asked me if I was going back to television, my answer would simply be, "I don't know; maybe someday. But right now I'm focused on writing and finishing my book." I had that thought in my head for quite some time, but I couldn't seem to commit to delivering the words. I worried that people would think writing a book with no guaranteed income was foolish. I worried that if I didn't say I was going back to TV, people would be disappointed that I had chosen a less glamorous career. I worried that I wasn't being responsible if I didn't hold a nine-to-five job at a large company with a 401(k) plan and benefits. And I worried that some people might think that my dream of publishing a book was just a silly pipe dream.

I was a bundle of worry. And my worry had a common theme. I was worried about what other people would think. For years I claimed that I didn't care what others thought. And now I had to call my own bullshit. I discovered that I wasn't committing to my professional dream because of what others might think. I also feared that I might fail. And when I got past the thought of failure, I worried that I might not be able to handle the path I was taking. In other words, I feared success. And because of this, I placed my goals in limbo. That sounds like such a waste of energy, doesn't it? Holding yourself back because of someone else's opinion? Fear that you might not be able to handle success? People do it all the time. Maybe you're doing it now when you think about your goals and dreams. And it doesn't matter what age you are because it happens at all ages. If you're reading this book and I'm describing you, accept this truth—*you* are the only person getting in your way. Yes, there are hurdles. Yes, there are setbacks. Yes, people will tell you no and you can't. But if you're dreaming it, then commit to the dream. Put the work into your dream. And fight your way through the limits and challenges that others have placed on you and that you have placed on yourself.

The moment the life coach sat across from me and told me that I clearly had a plan, a goal, and the skills to accomplish my dream, I was released from my own limbo. I was now committed to my goal. My goal was to write, finish, and publish my book. Once I committed to this goal, it was very easy for me to communicate it with confidence to anyone who asked about the direction of my professional life. I was keeping my dream alive. I was not giving up on my passion. I'm not sure that I actually had the eye of a tiger, but I was focused and determined!

While I was committed to my goal, there was still a "but." I was raised in a very traditional household. My parents were from the baby boomer generation. My father was a dentist. My mother was a nurse who eventually became a stay-at-home mom. My dad left for work in the morning and was home for dinner by five o'clock every night. My parents' career paths were very clear cut, as long as they passed all of their exams and earned their degrees. There was always steady income. We all had health insurance. And my father saved for a retirement plan. I didn't know what my traditional, conservative parents would think of their daughter's plan to live off the little money she had saved to write a book, which would not bring in a weekly paycheck. Every time my dad asked me, "What did you do today?" I held my breath before I responded, "I worked on my book." He might not admit it, but I'm sure my dad wanted me to be looking for a traditional job with a weekly paycheck. In fact, one morning when I logged onto my parents' computer, there was an article that was still open on the home screen. The article was titled, "When Should Parents Stop Helping Their Grown Kids Financially?"

At this point I was still paying all of my major bills. But yes, there were some things that my parents helped out with, like groceries, health insurance, and allowing me to stay in their home rent free. And there is no doubt about it—when you're financially supported by someone in any way, they make your business their business. My parents said they were supportive of my professional decisions, but I couldn't help but sense a judgmental tone from time to time. I was embarrassed when I saw that article and I momentarily questioned my path. Truth be told, I inherently lean toward the traditional route as well. I am not a risk taker. I am a product of how I was raised. Traditional. Logical. Safe. But while my upbringing was some-what controlled, what could not be controlled was my heart's desire to write. And I hoped that my writing would have a broad impact on others. So while logic told me to send out my resume and look for a job in public relations or continue to knock on the doors of television stations around the country, my soul was pushing me in a different direction.

Have you had a dream but thought it might sound silly? Does your dream take you out of your comfort zone? Has your brain been trained to think one way, but new thoughts creep in and derail your initial "brain training?" When this started happening to me, I decided to seek out the stories of mavericks. A maverick is someone who exhibits great independence in thought and action. A maverick does not conform to established standards. A maverick is a risk taker. I was not a maverick. But I was fascinated by those who lived their professional lives this way. I sought out these people. I asked them questions. And then I did more listening than I did talking. I was curious to know what they did with feelings of doubt and fear. I wondered if they worried about money. I wanted to know how they defined success. I wondered how they reacted when people told them no. I wanted to know what motivated them. These people were inherently the opposite of me. I always tend to play it safe. But I wondered if I could teach myself how to be a maverick. Could I take risks to make my dreams my reality? One thing I knew for sure was that I was in charge of my own limits. I could either choose to place limitations on myself or to remove the limitations. This is a choice we can all make.

I discovered during my conversations with risk takers that they had no fear. They were not afraid of failure at all. In fact, they found the word "failure" to be unacceptable. When they had setback after setback, the risk takers used their passion and resourcefulness to work around, underneath, and over their setbacks. When they were told no, they viewed the person or group who didn't support their goals as people who were just getting in their way and would later regret not saying yes. When I asked risk takers about their desire for money, their answers surprised me. Most, if not all of them, said that they were not driven by money. They were driven by their passion. They all felt that success was defined by completing the mission of their passion. They were not following their passion because of money.

That's a tough concept to accept in a materialistic world. We all have bills to pay. Cars we want to drive. Homes we want to inhabit. Name brands we want to wear. Is it possible to make money when you're not driven by money? My conversations with risk takers were unscientific, but I found that the answer was yes. Those who followed their passion were rewarded greatly. They were financially successful. Although sometimes they risked everything in pursuit of their dream, which left them broke at one time or another. But none of these mavericks felt that money was their greatest reward. I'm sure there are many entrepreneurs who would say that this concept sounds nice but that it's unrealistic. But this isn't a chapter about how to make money. This is a chapter about defining your passion, fighting against the limits that hold you back, saying *yes* to your goals and *no* to your fears.

What stops us from tackling a new opportunity? What holds us back from accomplishing our goals? Why don't we follow through on our dreams? Why do great ideas sit in our minds as nothing but ideas with no action? It's because of fear. For some it may be the fear of failure. For others it may be a fear of success. We get in our own way so many times in life. We have a dream to do something extraordinary, but we talk ourselves out of it through logical thinking. We say things like, "What if I can't handle it? What if I'm not good enough? What if I let someone down? What if I let myself down? What if I can't pay my bills? What if other people think I'm crazy for wanting to do x, y, or z? What if the grass isn't really greener on the other side? What if I make a mistake? What if this turns out to be a bad decision?" Maybe you're noticing a trend in these questions. They all start with "what if." I made a decision in my life to stop playing "what-ifs." Why? Because "what-ifs" aren't real. They are story lines that you make up in your mind.

We participate in "what-if" thoughts and conversations to predict the future. We're playing a guessing game with our own lives. I learned from successful mavericks that if you have a dream, commit to it. Follow through on the steps it takes to accomplish your goals. Live your dream. Talk about your dream. Talk about it with certainty, as though it's absolutely, without a doubt going to happen. Visualize it happening. See it. And believe it.

Live the passion in your playlist. Find the music that motivates you when other people's opinions get in your way. Listen to the words that feed the hunger inside of you to not give up on your dreams. And every time you start to get comfortable, weak, lazy, or find yourself making excuses, start playing that music again. Get off your rear and make things happen for yourself! You're in the driver's seat of your life. Stay the course. Don't pull off the road. Push "play." And keep living your playlist.

fourteen

The Power of Your Army

Playlist Song & Artist: "Little Wonders" Rob Thomas

Let your clarity define you. It's a sentiment that Rob Thomas sings about in the song "Little Wonders." And it's a phrase I say to myself almost daily. Our lives become overloaded with chaos. Our judgment can become clouded. And our intentions can be derailed. If you push your way through all of the muck and yuck, it's easier to focus on your clarity. When you focus on your clarity, you'll understand your own truths. For example, if you didn't get that promotion at work, then you either have more to learn in your current position or you need to look for a new job that will advance your talents. If that person you were madly in love with decided that he or she no longer wanted to date you, then that person was not the right match for you. You want to be with someone who feels the same way about you that you feel about him or her. Accept nothing less than that. If a friend turns his back on you, then he is no longer a friend. You do not want that person in your life. Stop *thinking* about what once was or what could be. Have clarity in the hurdles that you face. Allow the hurdles to advance your growth, not weaken it.

When I focused on my own clarity, I was able to better understand the issues that I struggled with for a long time. I accepted that it was okay that I lost my job. It was management's right to make the decision to eliminate my position. Employers have a right to change their minds, hire who they want, and go in a different direction. I finally had clarity on that fact and more. I wasn't happy where I was working. I was comfortable and complacent. I wasn't moving forward or being challenged, which is something I've always desired. It was time for me to move on. And when relationships in my life came to an end, of course I felt pain. And sometimes I fought the ending of those relationships. I often wanted the relationships to work out so badly that I overlooked that they were bad relationships. There should be no room in your life for unhealthy relationships. They are toxic. They cause you to feel emotions that are hurtful and sometimes embarrassing. You should never want to be with someone who makes you feel bad. If a person makes you feel bad, he or she is not a friend, and he or she is certainly not the kind of person you want as a partner. I always found that when I reached a point of clarity in bad relationships, it was easier to walk away.

Letting go is very difficult. Whether it's letting go of someone you love, letting go of a grudge, letting go of the past, or letting go of pain that you feel in your heart and soul. I'm still not sure that I've mastered the art of letting go. But I was tested at the end of one summer that I'll never forget. And I discovered at the end of that summer the key formula to letting go...

He (who shall remain nameless) and I met years before we started dating. Our first meeting was a quick exchange. Hellos, some pleasantries, and a friendly good-bye. The exchange was quick. It was a brief and forgettable conversation. It's possible that I noticed he was handsome, but I was so distracted by my own life that I didn't pay close attention to him. We crossed paths a couple years later at a charity event. I noticed that I caught his eye. I looked away quickly, feeling shy that his eyes were upon me. But moments after I looked away, I couldn't help but glance in his direction again. His eyes caught mine. But this time it was different. I didn't look away. We just stared at each other and smiled. When our eyes locked, it felt as if we were looking into each other's souls. This time I noticed how handsome he looked. And the more I looked at him, the more attracted to him I felt. We seemed to do a dance with our eyes in slow motion, just staring at each other from across the room. Until eventually we met, exchanged a handshake, and sat together in endless conversation for the rest of the night. He was funny and charming, not the least bit full of himself. Yet he also had an air of confidence. He came from humble beginnings but through hard work had found success in his profession. And while he had to wear a suit by day, he preferred his favorite T-shirt and old beat-up shorts that he wore every time he went fishing. He was a little older than me, and the wisdom from the years that he lived drew me closer to him. Our lives were separately busy. But we spent as many hours together as we could with our demanding schedules. And the time we spent together was well spent. We would often say that we could make the most out of just two minutes together. Some days, we would brown bag a lunch, buy a bottle of cheap wine, and drive until we found a park bench to laugh the afternoon away. Or we might meet up at a local dive bar that we would refer to as "that place on the corner." We would suck down a few vodka sodas and then fill up on a large pepperoni pizza—always New York style! Every week we would take a yoga class together. Even though he had an athletic build, I thought his tall frame would seem uncoordinated doing yoga poses. But his competitive spirit mastered a handstand long before I did. While the purpose of the yoga classes were to do something good for our bodies, the best part for me was the moment at the end of class when we were lying still on our backs and his hand reached over to touch mine. It was sensual. It was sweet. It was pure and simple romance.

But our favorite place to spend time together was at a local park not far from where I grew up. There was a long trail in the park. And we loved taking walks together. This was the place where I believed we became soul mates. During these walks, we shared our most intimate thoughts, our greatest dreams, our biggest worries, and our regrets. We laughed, we cried, we kissed. Every emotion was filled with passion. And still, when he would look into my eyes, I was fixed on his gaze. I couldn't take my eyes off of him. Actually, I didn't want to take my eyes off of him. I knew that with every step and every exchange, I was falling in love with this man. And I felt the same kind of love from him. In those moments, nothing else existed. I wanted to stay right there, hand in hand, locked in those moments. He came with a past, like most people do. But it didn't scare me or turn me away. I knew how I felt about him. And I trusted how he felt about me. We were in love. Eventually we talked about a life together. Getting married. Having children. We thought about where we would live. We covered all of the basics and more. We met each other's families. And everyone was on board. This was everything I dreamed of. I felt like the luckiest girl in the world. I could see my future. He was my future. And it looked really good.

Right up until it didn't. Something about this man suddenly changed. He talked differently. He looked at me differently. Even the text messages he would send me seemed like a different person was writing them. What was I missing? Did I do something wrong that I was unaware of? What was happening to my once perfect relationship? I knew something was wrong. I could feel it in my gut. But I didn't want to admit that this relationship was changing for the worse. And then one day, just like that, he was gone. He told me that he changed his mind. He didn't want a future with me. I was crushed. I would like to say I felt blindsided, except I sensed a change not long before he ended our relationship. I felt as if I had no closure because my feelings had not changed, and I was confused as to why his did. I was left with unanswered questions, such as, "How could you leave me after you told me that you loved me? I shared my soul with you. How could you turn your back on me? You made promises to me. Were they all lies? Why don't you want me?" The questions were endless. Some of them were repetitive. And none of them had the answer that I wanted. I hoped the answer would be that he made a mistake in leaving me. I wanted him to tell me that I was the best thing that ever happened to him. But that answer never came. And I couldn't get past the idea that in one summer I fell in love. And then he was gone. Something so wonderful was over in one season. I felt worthless. I felt ashamed. I felt pathetic at times. I felt unloved. I felt lonely without him. And then I came face to face with the key formula of letting go. It was something that was always around me. And it was mighty. I like to refer to it as my army.

I fell in love with a man one summer day. And at the end of that summer, he was gone and left me questioning my own worth. I felt as if my world had come to an end. I didn't want to get out of bed in the morning. I cried all the time. And I kept replaying our good times over and over in my mind, which left me confused about why he changed his mind. After taking a walk alone on a different trail in the park, I gained some clarity. Before I met this man, I was a strong woman. I was vibrant and happy. I laughed often and loved fully. I was confident and did my best to carry myself with grace and pride every day. I was this person because my parents raised me to be that kind of woman. And I realized that my family and friends loved me for all of my good and bad parts. The loving people in my life built me up over many years. It became clear during my walk that I could not allow this one man to defeat the army of love I had around me my entire life.

My army was strong. So strong, in fact, that they would not only protect me from a hurtful man, but they would help me conquer all of the other destructive people and situations in my life. My army stood beside me and said, "Go ahead, take away her job, try to break her down, betray her trust, make her cry tears of worry, try to strip her confidence...We will guard and protect her from all of it. And if she falls, we will support her. And if she needs to be carried, we will pick her up."

And just when any of the demons thought that they won, my army reminded me that I'm strong, wise, gifted, kind and loving, thoughtful and caring, and a woman who will not be beaten. My army reminded me that I can stand up and say I learned something from you, but you did not win this battle. While the hurtful experiences in my life fed my weaknesses, my army fed my strengths. And my strengths won.

Winning your own personal battles takes time. And it's important to have the strength of others whom you trust. Strength doesn't have to come in numbers for this kind of battle, it just has to come in the form of unconditional love from someone you can trust with your soul. My army of strength started with my mom, Karen, and my dad, Ray, my brother, Paul, and sister, Kathleen, other family members, and some amazing friends. The process of healing took a lot of help from my family and friends. But through their loving words, their encouragement, and their patience, I slowly became whole again. I learned that it's possible to work through the pain, work out the grudges, and come out a better person. The process of healing helps you to learn more about yourself. But the healing can't be rushed. You have to feel the pain in order to heal. That takes time. And some wounds leave scars. But those scars are reminders of how far you've come and what you've learned along the way. They show you how strong you really are. Scars remind you that the hardest part is over and that you survived.

When you make it through your struggles in life, you'll enjoy the good parts even more. When you're ready to let go of the pain and gain clarity about your struggles, the things that used to bother you will no longer consume you. This is when you'll begin to find peace. And if you choose to start living your playlist, don't just listen to the words in the music. Be sure to listen to the words that your army speaks to you. In time, you'll find that as you absorb their loving, wise, and encouraging words, you'll find your own voice. And then let the clarity of your voice define your actions and the person that you want to be.

As I was getting ready to end this book, I wondered if I needed to wait a few more years to write a perfectly packaged ending. I wanted to write about the amazing job I had landed and the wonderful man that I had married. But I realized on this journey, life isn't perfect. And neither are all endings. Often things don't go as planned. Sometimes our script in life encounters writer's block. I'm learning that this is okay. Stop putting pressure on yourself to live out the script that someone else wrote for you, or maybe even the one you wrote for yourself ten or twenty years ago. But don't ever stop challenging yourself. Continue to seek wisdom from others. Don't settle for people, places, or things that make you unhappy. Choose your army wisely. And don't be afraid to kick people out of your army when they aren't playing for your team anymore. Pray for clarity in your life. And know that clarity will give you answers. And LIVE YOUR PLAYLIST! I promise it will help you get through your shit one song at a time. May you laugh, dance, feel empowered, and rock on every time you push "play"!

Acknowledgements

"We Are Family"

To my parents, Karen and Ray Vecchio. Thank you for your patience during this long journey. You allowed my words and thoughts to marinate and become stories that healed me. I'm so blessed to have your unconditional love and support. Your wisdom and strength always guide me. I love you forever.

To my sister, Kathleen. My adviser. You are my best friend. Thank you for your genuine heart and always believing the best in me. Your faith in me was a constant force that kept me moving forward. I'm so blessed to have you as my sister.

To my brother, Paul. You showed me that I was not alone on this journey. Thank you for teaching me the meaning of "thou mayest." Your lessons stay with me always. I'm so thankful that you are in my life. You are the perfect brother.

To Nonnie and Grandpa Bill, Grandma Mary and Grandpa Hank. You created our family's strong foundation. Thank you for making all of my family memories happy ones. I love you.

To Amanda, thank you for reminding me to "shake it out" and for the happy times with a bottle of bubbly! To Angelo, thank you for being one of my biggest fans!

To Anna, Amelia, Adriana, Lauren, Henry, and Nicholas. You will always be precious to me and give me a reason to smile every day. My heart is happy when I'm with you.

"Thank You for Being a Friend"
Dominique Moceanu...I'm honored that you would write such a beautiful foreword to my book. Your words truly make my heart smile. You are an inspiration, a beautiful person, and a true blessing. The heavens were on my side when we became friends; you are an angel in my life. Thank you for challenging me to be raw and vulnerable through my writing. Thank you for believing in my message. And thank you for coaching me to be an empowered woman. Your friendship has made me a better person.

Lori Stevic-Rust...A dream in my mind became an active goal because of a phone conversation we had one summer afternoon. You pushed me. You encouraged me. You protected me. And you guided me to dig deeper through my writing. I love you and your family. Thank you for always making me feel as if your home is my home.

I will always cherish and be thankful for these friends who picked me up when I was down. Gave me strength when I was weak. Encouraged my writing. Listened to my writing. And taught me the importance of living my playlist...

Jennifer Kryz Sommers, you've been my rock and confidante. Thank you for hanging onto my shirt during the falls, pushing me during the climbs, and celebrating me during my successes. Diana Fusco, you are the definition of a strong woman who supports smart women. I love your feisty spirit, but I'm grateful for your generous soul. Melody Clemens, with you there are always laughs and filled glasses! Thank you for making me feel like a rock star when I couldn't find the beat. Jen Shoppach, some of my most memorable life moments happened with you. We met Paul McCartney together! Thank you for the many care packages and unforgettable trips!

To Timothy L. Kiedrowski, my marketing and public relations mastermind. You answered every phone call. You met every challenge. You are a friend, a supporter, and wise beyond your years. Thank you for setting this up to be a fun ride!

To my creative team, thank you for your talent and passion. Colleen Reiner, in this case a book can be judged by your cover. It's perfect! Eric Mull, you are brilliant with a lens! Everything you shoot is cover worthy. I'll always be grateful to *Cleveland Magazine* for bringing you into my world.

And to the following friends who were pivotal during my journey as I wrote this book. Thank you for your love, guidance, and heartfelt friendship...Jason Roberts, Michael Canales, Mike Panigutti, Danialle Lynce, Mike Chase, Dina Rodriguez, Angela Presti, Delories McCall, Kathy Dawson, Maureen Kyle, Rachel McCoy, Annie Thomas, Jan Jones, Shelly Artz, Shane "Rover" French, Carolyn Brown, Dave Koz, Taylor Johnson, Larry Walker, Maggie Jones, Beverly Maloney-Fischback and Joel Reichlin.

To the people of Cleveland. Thank you for your support and for always rooting for me!

And to my coach. You know who you are. Thank you for teaching me that even the best fall down sometimes. And then they get back up. I will be forever grateful to you and the role that you played in my life.

"You're So Vain"
For those who think this book is about them.

CPSIA information can be obtained at www.ICGtesting.com
Printed in the USA
BVOW04s0155261214

380872BV00018BA/669/P

9 780692 289044